Effective
Time-Management Techniques
for School Administrators

Effective
TIME-MANAGEMENT
TECHNIQUES
for School Administrators

Neil J. Shipman

Jack B. Martin

A. Bruce McKay

Robert E. Anastasi

Prentice-Hall, Inc.   Englewood Cliffs, New Jersey

Prentice-Hall International, Inc., *London*
Prentice-Hall of Australia, Pty. Ltd., *Sydney*
Prentice-Hall Canada, Inc., *Toronto*
Prentice-Hall of India Private Ltd., *New Delhi*
Prentice-Hall of Japan, Inc., *Tokyo*
Prentice-Hall of Southeast Asia Pte. Ltd., *Singapore*
Whitehall Books, Ltd., *Wellington, New Zealand*
Editora Prentice-Hall do Brasil Ltda., *Rio de Janeiro*

© 1983 by
Leadership Training Associates
Silver Spring, Maryland

Library of Congress Cataloging in Publication Data
Main entry under title:

Effective time-management techniques for school
   administrators.

   Bibliography: p.
   Includes index.
    1. School administrators—Addresses, essays, lectures.
2. Time management—Addresses, essays, lectures.
I. Shipman, Neil J.
LB2831.6.E39 1983   371.2   82-21611

ISBN 0-13-246488-8

Printed in the United States of America

ABOUT THE AUTHORS

The coauthors of *Effective Time-Management Techniques for School Administrators* bring over 60 years of cumulative experience as practicing administrators to their subject. All are currently serving as administrators in the Montgomery County, Maryland, public schools and are also active as consultants. In 1980, they established Leadership Training Associates, which offers a wide range of consulting services to school systems.

Neil J. Shipman, Ed.D., University of Southern California, is principal of Fox Chapel School and the immediate past president of the Elementary School Administrators Association of Montgomery County. Dr. Shipman has taught at all levels and has consulted with a number of school systems on goal setting, supervision and evaluation of staff, and leadership styles.

Jack B. Martin, M.Ed., Western Maryland College, has been a school principal in Montgomery County since 1968 and is most recently principal of Harmony Hills Elementary School. Mr. Martin is a past president of the Montgomery County Elementary School Administrators Association. He was a consultant on a Florida State study of children of migrant workers and has done consulting work in Maryland and West Virginia on leadership styles and time and stress management.

A. Bruce McKay, Ed.D., University of Massachusetts, is in the Department of Staff Development in the Montgomery County schools and has had wide administrative and teaching experience at all levels. Dr. McKay carried out the planning and conceptual development of a comprehensive training program for a staff of 650 management personnel in the county schools and has served as a management consultant to many districts across the country.

Robert E. Anastasi, Ed.D., University of Southern Mississippi, is principal of Rosemont Elementary School. Dr. Anastasi is an active member of national, state, and local administrators organizations and is a past president of the Maryland Association of Elementary School Administrators. He has consulted in several school systems on negotiation rights, supervision and evaluation of staff, time management, and leadership styles.

ACKNOWLEDGMENTS

We greatly appreciate the assistance of our very able typist, Leslie Martin Moore. Her assistance as a critical reader, not only a typist, was extremely valuable.

Of course, without the support and patience of our wives, Sandy, Sue, Suzie, and Wanda, we could never have finished this product.

We want to publicly thank each other for the contributions, positive criticism, and patience with one another. Writing a book by "committee" is difficult, but, as evident, not impossible.

We would also like to thank the following people and schools for their contributions:

Fagen, Stanley, *Checklist for Developing an Effective School Discipline Approach.*

Mark Twain School, Rockville, Maryland, *Rights And Responsibilities of Members of the Mark Twain Community.*

McKenzie, F., *Some Thoughts on Classroom Control.*

Montgomery County Public Schools, In-Service Course, MT-04, *Behavior Management.*

Thomas S. Wootton High School, Rockville, Maryland, Figures 5-4, 5-9, 5-10 and 5-12 in Chapter 5.

Parkland Junior High School, Rockville, Maryland, *Plans for Curriculum Improvement.*

THE PRACTICAL VALUE OF THIS BOOK

Today, we school administrators are being asked to take charge of local implementation of federal legislation and state curriculum programs for basic education and accountability. We are expected to manage declining school enrollments and see to it that educational equity becomes a reality. We principals and other school personnel are expected to carry out new curricular approaches at all levels, handle society's drug and alcohol problems, take care of school discipline, provide sex education, manage early childhood programs, coordinate free lunches for retired citizens, monitor dog and human vaccination and other health programs, and provide a model of hope for our future citizens in a world where optimism and positive thinking are being severely tested.

This book will:

- help you set priorities in meeting the complex challenges school administrators face,
- give you specific techniques to cope with difficult and time-consuming tasks,
- help you decide on the most productive way to spend your time,
- suggest organizational patterns that will make time more productive,
- help you delegate responsibility more effectively and handle routine tasks more efficiently,
- provide you with the tools to manage your job and not be harnessed to it, and
- reinforce and rekindle your sense of mission, your faith in education, and your belief in your own ability to be an agent for changing and improving the education of our young people.

The promise of this book is that you will find sound advice in straightforward terms with tips and strategies for managing time efficiently. For example, forms, charts, and illustrations will be numerous to *save your time* rather than forcing you to get the same information from the proverbial 1,000 words.

This is an answer book, a problem solver, and an ideas book that deals specifically with the needs of busy administrators. It has a what-to-do and how-to-do-it format, including anecdotes and specific guidelines for you to follow.

All nine chapters include many specific, proven time-management ideas. The book offers techniques and insights regarding:

- being effective, instead of just being busy,
- structuring your time-management style,
- making your environment work for you,
- dealing with overload,

11

- establishing time-saving procedures in working with student discipline,
- using time-saving techniques in selecting, supervising, and evaluating staff,
- maximizing output through minimizing time spent in meetings and conferences,
- saving time when working with all facets of the organization, and
- designing your own time-management system.

The final chapter, "Now You Can Design Your Own Time-Management System," incorporates a special format to help identify steps to improve your personal time-management style for your on-the-job needs. Here, you will personally organize your time-management plan by incorporating your choice of practical strategies offered in the first eight chapters, such as:

- reserving a specific time *each day* to separate daily mail, read it, and prepare responses,
- developing a daily "to do" list and doing the *most important* items, rather than the easiest, first,
- setting personal goals at least monthly, establishing a time line for their achievement, and keeping track of your progress toward them,
- keeping your desk clear and organizing your office with only essential items in the desk drawers or a nearby file, and
- establishing a routine with your secretary including screening the mail, preparing certain written communications, and keeping your calendar.

This book was written to help principals and other school administrators. We have packed it with practical, tested ideas and techniques for managing time wisely. The costs for not taking charge of our time, for losing control over what we do and how we work, for complaining, and being cynical about our job are too great for us, our staffs, and the students we hope to help. By reading this book, you will learn ways to master your time and renew your conviction that your work can truly make a difference.

Neil J. Shipman
Jack B. Martin
A. Bruce McKay
Robert E. Anastasi

Effective
Time-Management Techniques
for School Administrators

CONTENTS

4

WHAT TO DO ABOUT OVERLOAD 85

5

ESTABLISHING TIME-SAVING PROCEDURES IN WORKING WITH
SCHOOL DISCIPLINE 95

6

TIME-SAVING TECHNIQUES IN SELECTING, SUPERVISING, AND
EVALUATING STAFF 115

7

MAXIMIZING OUTPUT BY MINIMIZING TIME SPENT IN MEETINGS AND CONFERENCES 133

8

HOW TO SAVE TIME WHEN WORKING WITH ALL FACETS OF THE ORGANIZATION 149

9

NOW YOU CAN DESIGN YOUR OWN TIME-MANAGEMENT SYSTEM 161

TIME-MANAGEMENT AIDS

19

Chapter 1

Being Effective Instead of Just Being Busy

*He that will not apply new remedies must expect
new evils; for time is the greatest innovator—Francis Bacon*

INTRODUCTION

There are four steps involved in studying the time structure of one's work day. First, become familiar with time-management techniques. Second, analyze present time-management practices. Third, decide what needs to be changed to help you be effective instead of just busy. Fourth, design and implement procedures to accomplish the desired time-management changes.

Changes in our time-management styles occur only when we are motivated and ready to adopt new patterns of behavior. Lewin calls this phase of change unfreezing or the "thawing-out" when forces acting on us are rearranged to enable us to see the need for change.[1] We then adopt new behaviors by modeling others' behavior (identification) or by being placed in a situation where we must adopt new behaviors to be successful (internalization). As principals, we have all modeled behaviors learned in training sessions and internalized other new behaviors when needed in order to implement new policies. We have seen the greatest changes of time-management styles when there is a combination of identification and internalization. In this chapter we want you to identify with us as principals and internalize those suggestions that will help you implement your new time-management policies.

CHARACTERISTICS OF TIME

Time is the one commodity that is unbiased, available to all in equal amounts, does not cost us anything monetarily, and is completely at our own disposal. Rowan says we cannot store it, we cannot spend it in advance, we never seem to have enough of it, and we cannot retrieve it once it is used.[2] The main difference to each of us is the way we use the time that is available.

---

[1]K. Lewin, "Frontiers in Group Dynamics: Concept, Method, and Reality in Social Science; Social Equilibria and Social Change." *Human Relations*, 1947, *1*, 5–41.

[2]R. Rowan, "Keeping the Clock from Running Out." *Fortune*, 1978, 98, 76–78.

Time is a ready and all-too-frequently-used excuse for not accomplishing an assigned task—

"Gosh, my time ran out."

"Man, time flies when you're having fun."

"Wow, where'd all the time go?"

"I can't get to it right now because I don't have enough time"—ad nauseam.

As practicing school administrators, we know that under most circumstances, principals and other school management personnel should be able to fulfill their responsibilities within a reasonable work week of 40 to 50 hours. We all have available to us 60 seconds every hour, 8 hours every day, 5 days every week, and 4 or 5 weeks every month—and we should be able to manage our job in the time available to us. If we cannot, then the problem, most likely, lies in our personal lack of management skills.

We cannot control actual time because the hands of the clock continue to move beyond our control. However, we are each capable of deciding what to do with our time so that it becomes not a question of how to control time, but rather how best to organize ourselves within our available time frame.[3]

We have identified several "time kinds":

a. work time

b. worry time

c. leisure time

d. free time

e. prime (or peak) time

f. busy time

g. sleep time

Work time is normally comprised of certain set hours each day, for example, 8:00 A.M. to 5:00 P.M. The key to effectiveness may lie in how much of this time actually is devoted to work activity that is intended to accomplish major goals of your job.

Worry time gains no one anything and should be converted to another of the time kinds.

Leisure time should be built into each day to help ensure productiveness of work time. The old axiom, "All work and no play makes Jack a dull boy," may also make Jack an ineffective principal.

Free time should not be equated with leisure time or any of the other time kinds. We are in no way advocating that your entire day be scheduled. Free time may be used in a variety of ways. For example, use your free time to read that best seller you have been wanting to get to for weeks.

If you analyze a time log like the one shown in Figure 1-1, p. 27, your own prime or peak time period should be identified and used to concentrate on your highest priority. (Setting priorities as a major component of time management is discussed in Chapter 2.)

Busy time equates with "phony time." How often do you feel the need to prove to others how busy you are? You can show them best by using work time most productively.

---

[3]R. Alec Mackenzie, *The Time Trap.* New York: American Management Assn., Inc., 1972.

Sleep time is really very important. There is little doubt that insufficient rest causes errors, inefficiency, and ineffectiveness. A brief 10-minute nap or rest-and-relaxation period when tired may increase effectiveness many times over. Of course, resting 10 minutes to every 5 minutes worked may lead to an early and unexpected retirement—so be careful!

IDENTIFYING YOUR OWN TIME WASTERS

Since our aim is to become more effective through better management of our time, it is imperative that activities considered major time wasters be identified. Time wasters, in our opinion, are inefficient procedures for handling tasks that must be done or dealing with items personally that could be done just as well, or better, by others. Take a few minutes, and on a blank piece of paper, jot down four or five items you consider major time wasters.

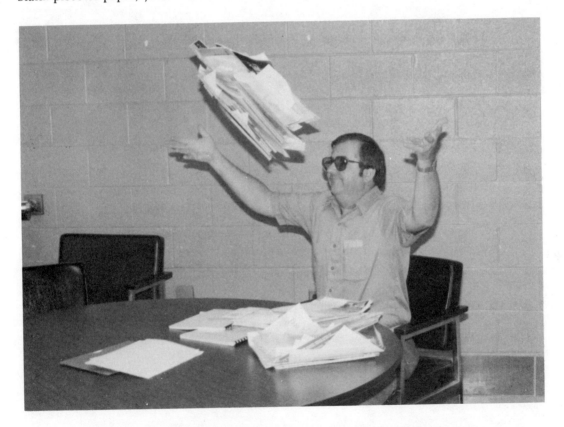

The frustration of dealing with junk mail has been felt by all administrators and is one of our greatest time wasters.

You have just accomplished the vital first step in getting control of your time.

What are major time wasters as identified by administrators like yourselves? In a poll reported by Powers, the ten worst time wasters as perceived by more than fifty chairmen of boards and presidents and vice-presidents of corporations were:

1. Telephones
2. Mail
3. Meetings
4. Public Relations
5. Paperwork
6. Commuting
7. Business lunches
8. Civic Duties
9. Incompetents
10. Family Demands[4]

Mackenzie identified the following 15 leading time wasters based on experiences of managers in 15 countries:

1. Telephone interruptions
2. Drop-in visitors
3. Meetings—scheduled as well as unscheduled
4. Crisis situations for which planning ahead was not possible
5. Lack of objectives, priorities, or deadlines
6. Cluttered desk and personal disorganization
7. Involvement in routine and detail that should be delegated
8. Attempting too much at one time and underestimating the time it takes to do it
9. Failure to set up clear lines of responsibility and authority
10. Inadequate, inaccurate, or delayed information from others
11. Indecision and procrastination
12. Lack of clear communication and instruction
13. Inability to say no
14. Lack of standards and progress reports (we educators would probably call that "accountability")
15. Fatigue[5]

A variety of factors such as group dynamics, leadership styles, and organizational expectations could result in other time wasters, such as

---

[4] R. C. Powers, *Identifying the Community Power Structure.* (North Central Regional Extension Publication No. 19, NCRS-5 Leadership Series No. 2). Ames, Iowa: Iowa State University of Science and Technology, 1965.
[5] R. Mackenzie, *The Time Trap.*

1. Errors (yours and others)
2. Buying into personal problems of staff
3. Improper attention to priorities
4. Concern about problems over which you have no control
5. Incomplete planning
6. Poorly organized secretary
7. Junk mail
8. Socializing
9. Insufficient knowledge
10. Use of inappropriate leadership style
11. Inadequate supervision of staff
12. Poor conferencing/interviewing techniques
13. Coping poorly with stress
14. Government regulations
15. Rumor mill
16. Reports
17. Failure to complete tasks
18. Poor self-discipline
19. Open-door policy

Throughout this book, a variety of techniques to combat these time wasters are discussed.

USING TIME-MANAGEMENT TECHNIQUES TO OVERCOME TIME WASTERS

Set Goals!

A major problem often faced by school administrators is over-involvement. Since educational management involves working with and through people, we suffer sometimes from spending too much time in meetings, on the phone, handling parent or teacher complaints, and in other "people-related" activities. It is important that we carry out these responsibilities with grace and good human relations, but it should not be necessary to spend all of our time in such activities. In fact, the amount of time spent in such activities could be reduced by as much as one-third.

To do so, there should be a clear understanding of the purpose (goal) of the activity. Constantly remind yourself when you are in a tedious meeting or lengthy telephone discussion of its *purpose* or *goal*. "Why am I having the meeting?" "What am I trying to achieve during this phone call?" "Am I spending my time in the way that will best move me toward my goal?" This will help to redirect the activity as well as prevent the irretrievable loss of time in idle conversation or irrelevant trivia.

Do It!

All of us have certain tasks we like to do and those that we avoid with a passion. While many of the things we disdain are indeed troublesome, we must learn to control them and not be controlled *by* them. We must face unpleasant tasks or assignments with two important attitudes. First, we should try to tackle them rather than avoid them through procrastination. Unpleasant tasks should be attempted not with constant complaining, but with a positive attitude, unless one wants others to see him as a complainer. Second, such tasks should be attempted with as much efficiency as possible. This means work to get the *maximum* results with the *minimum* effort. Do the job, do it right, do it as efficiently as possible, but get it done—NOW!

DOING SOMETHING ABOUT YOUR OWN TIME WASTERS

For most managers, the usual time wasters include those listed earlier in this chapter such as meetings, telephone, procrastination, and time-consuming forms. As you begin to address your concerns about your personal management of time, it will be necessary for you to *spend* some time to *save* some time. You will have to examine your management style objectively. One effective means of doing this is to keep a daily time log for one week as illustrated in Figure 1-1.

Throughout this book, you will find many forms and checklists to help analyze use of time. There are also forms to help plan next steps. We suggest you copy these forms to keep in a loose-leaf notebook. In this way, you will be organized so that you may add and delete materials as you see fit. After completing the book and the materials, you will have in one place your own time-management design.

Another way to recognize your own time wasters is to identify some of the major categories of time wasters, those things that seem to dominate your energy and time. When you do this, we suggest you refer back to the time wasters identified on pages 24 and 25 and group them into two broad categories. First, try to list the major tasks or responsibilities of your job, and priority rank them in terms of those that are most time consuming or most difficult to manage. Second, decide which of the time wasters you identified are a result of your personal style of management and group these together. Now, try to generate a wide variety of ideas that would enable you to alleviate those time wasters. Try to focus on the things you can do about them. Develop a plan and stick to it. The main thing is to focus on those things you control or can influence. Remember, do not try to blame others or the organization. Just decide that you are going to try to make progress on your main problem area. Do not attempt too much. It is better to pick a few things and accomplish them than to make a grand plan and not do anything. In your notebook, use Figure 1-2, p. 28, to help with this.

Another way to examine your time-management problems is through the use of a questionnaire such as the one shown in Figure 1-3, p. 29. Try completing the form, responding to the items honestly; look at the items you marked "Never," and start planning how to deal with them.

Figure 1-1

DAILY TIME LOG

1. Record activities every 30 minutes.

2. Assess each activity's importance at the end of the day.

3. Following completion, analyze how the activity could have been better handled.

4. Compare activities with Daily Objectives Time Plan (Chapter 2).

5. Keep log for one week.

Date _____

TIME	ACTIVITY	PRIORITY 1. Most Important 2. Important 3. Not Important	ACTION (Examples: delegated, did myself, did not do)

Figure 1-2

TIME WASTERS

	Time Waster	Cause	Solution
1.			
2.			
3.			
4.			
5.			
6.			
7.			
8.			
9.			
10.			

Figure 1-3

TIME-MANAGEMENT ANALYSIS

Directions: Read each statement carefully. If you incorporate the action in your work at all times check "Always." If you find it convenient at times and not convenient at other times, check "Sometimes." If you don't use the action, check "Never."

	ALWAYS	SOMETIMES	NEVER
1. I know the time of the day when I am most effective. (Doing the right job right.)			
2. When I find that I have to wait for someone, I have a magazine, book, or other work-related materials available.			
3. During a lull or when I am engaged in a low-priority goal, I self-evaluate if I am using my time to *my* best advantage.			
4. I examine what has to be done during the day or week, place these in a priority list, start at the top, and work straight through the list.			
5. I have placed my life goals in priority and am aware of them.			
6. I critique the way I perform routine tasks to determine if there is a better way.			
7. I have established objectives that enable me to fulfill my Number 1 priority.			
8. I put my job-related thoughts on paper or a tape recorder.			
9. Rather than taking the time to read a professional journal or research report thoroughly, I scan it quickly for pertinent information or read the summary.			

Figure 1-3 (cont'd)

	ALWAYS	SOMETIMES	NEVER
10. I realize and accept that there are parts of the job I do not like to do or have failed to get around to.			
11. I keep in mind that the important things will always get done.			
12. I call in experts when they can be utilized to help provide a solution.			
13. I believe in and practice the old adage and make sure "the dog wags the tail" rather than "the tail wagging the dog."			
14. I break large, time-consuming projects into small, manageable tasks.			
15. My main goal is to use my time wisely and complete as much as possible in the time available.			
16. I devote a great deal of time to projects that will yield the most valuable long-run results.			
17. I am aware that some of my time is controlled by others and do not let this cause undue stress.			
18. I avoid stress by performing an unpleasant task immediately rather than procrastinating.			
19. I plan my time so that there is ample time for my family and me.			
20. I make sure there is enough time to complete the most important projects.			
21. I establish completion times for all projects, regardless of who will be working on them.			
22. The job of a school administrator is the most enjoyable job I can imagine.			
23. I handle all letters and memos only once.			
24. I avoid tasks that do not have any payoff.			
25. I utilize delegation to my best advantage.			

INTERPRETATION

If you checked a column "Always," you are utilizing good time-management skills in that particular area. A check in the "Sometimes" column indicates that you are discriminating in your approach. You may want to look at those more closely to determine if they should be moved to the "Always" column. To do this, follow the procedure below. A "Never" statement is indicative of poor time-management skills in those aspects of your job. List these on a separate piece of paper with a column headed "What to Do About It." In this column, list behaviors or activities you could employ to bring about a positive change.

Example:

Statement	What to Do About It
23. I handle all letters and memos only once.	1. Decide on first reading what action is required and write this action on the memo. 2. Decide who should deal with it and write that person's name on it. 3. Jot some ideas on it and let my secretary respond. 4. Handle each piece only one time.

Know Thy Role

Effective managers know and maintain their roles. During meetings, conferences, phone calls, and the like, you should avoid temptation to gripe about things that are beyond your control. Much time, as well as energy, can be wasted by complaining about school system policy or central office or the lousy board meeting or those stupid forms. The skillful manager recognizes his or her role within the overall organization, be it principal, executive staff, or even superintendent. In any case, you are a representative of the system, and as such, have to deal with peers, your superiors, and others who rely on you for leadership. Part of that responsibility is to know the boundaries within which you are to function in the organization. Know what the "givens" are. Know what latitude your role allows in decision making. Do not allow the group or others to waste time by trying to change policies or procedures that are not controlled by you. Remind others of the boundaries and restrictions, and of your role—of what you can do and what you cannot do.

Train Thyself

It takes a skillful manager to conduct a worthwhile meeting or conference or to handle a difficult phone call. School administrators could really profit from formal training workshops on such topics. However, this could also be accomplished through professional reading or by picking another manager who demonstrates these skills and watching the person in action to pick up new ideas or tips.

A support group could also be developed with colleagues. This group could have a few actual practice sessions simulating difficult communication problems. For example, 3-minute role plays could be done and then discussed. A video or audio recording of your behavior while conducting a meeting could be analyzed by yourself, your support group, or your staff, looking for instances where you were not moving toward your goal.

Regardless of what technique is used in self-training, three questions should predominate:

1. What should I *stop* doing in order to be more effective in using time?
2. What should I *start* doing in order to be more effective in using time?
3. What should I *continue* to do in order to be more effective in using time?

TIME-MANAGEMENT MYTHS

There are many ways we administrators try to rationalize our ineffective time-management techniques. Most of these rationalizations are in reality the myths that follow.

Myth—If I work 12 hours a day, I will be further ahead. As noted earlier, when the point of physical or mental fatigue is approached, one enters into the area of diminishing returns—the time when more effort is required to do a task, thus increasing the likelihood of error. In the long run, this will result in more time being spent to improve the quality and correct the mistakes. Clarence Randall, former chairman of Inland Steel, calls this the myth of the overworked executive. In reality, managers are only overworked because they want to be.

Myth—I have so much to do now, I cannot afford to take time for planning. By not planning for long-term goals and short-term objectives, you permit yourself to become the local fire brigade—in other words, you devote most of your time to fighting brush fires and reacting to crisis situations. Time must be spent in daily planning and organizing.

Myth—If it is to be done right, I must do it myself. It is simply not possible to do everything that is expected of a school administrator yourself. Accepting this myth automatically condemns you to the preceding first two myths. If you believe in the process used to select your subordinates, then honestly give them a chance to show what they can do and delegate to them as much as possible. Remember, your job is to get things done through other people.

Myth—I have to read every piece of mail and every report that comes into the office. This is not necessarily true. Learn to separate the important from the unimportant. Leave junk mail alone. Read only reports that are pertinent to your situation. Devote reading time to professional growth activities.

Myth—If I do not do anything, perhaps the problem will go away. It will not go away. A nondecision is still a decision. The entire time it is there, you will be subjecting yourself to undue stress and wasting valuable time thinking about it.

Myth—If I spend a lot of time accomplishing this task, it will increase my efficiency. All the time in the world spent on a task may still show ineffectiveness if it is spent on the wrong task at the wrong time and does not attain the desired outcome. Efficiency means doing the job right. Effectiveness means doing the *right* job right.

Myth—Since I am the principal, my time spent on making decisions will improve the quality of the decisions. Not so. One principle of effective management is that the best decisions are those made at the lowest level, providing good judgment and pertinent facts are present. For example, decisions about a class instructional program could be made by a competent classroom teacher, not the principal. On the other hand, principals should spend time helping less competent teachers improve their classroom practices.

Myth—I will be a more effective administrator if I have an open-door policy. Yes, it is important to be available to parents, teachers, students, and others with whom one works. However, this does not mean your office door should be physically open 24 hours a day. If this is happening, it is no wonder you have no time to work on your own priorities. You should build in times to plan, organize, and do other such things—in other words, "planned unavailability."

Myth—I simply do not have enough time. You do not have enough time or is it more that you do not best utilize the time that is available? After all, we all have the same total amount of time. Why is it that some managers appear to have more time than others? Time is fixed. It passes all at the same rate. It is only through poor time-management techniques that administrators are left with too much to do in too little time.

TROUBLESOME MANAGEMENT STYLES AND WHAT TO DO ABOUT THEM

There are many ways to look at personal management styles. Those time wasters discussed earlier in this chapter are indicative of troublesome management styles.

Another useful concept popularized during the transactional analysis movement is that of drivers.[6] Let us translate these "drivers" into management styles and see how they influence our way of dealing with time management.

The "be perfect" style of manager aims for perfection and sets the same expectations for his or her subordinates. Because of the need to be perfect, this person wastes valuable time on details, redoing tasks, and worrying about keeping up appearances. This manager wastes time on trivia and other low-yield activities.

The "hurry up" administrator always tries to do things faster. This is the one who answers questions before they are asked, finishes sentences for others, talks and moves rapidly—the finger drummer. This person tends to come to meetings late and then leave as though in a rush. A good time manager should never have to rush. This is the style of one who overschedules appointments and makes mistakes in paper work. This manager also has a tendency to fail to take the necessary time to explain tasks to others when delegating.

The manager whose style is "try harder" goes off on tangents, procrastinates, and repeats questions. He is always trying but never succeeding. This person comes to work early, leaves late, and usually takes home a full briefcase of work. He never completes projects in advance, always working to the deadline, and even then frequently missing it.

The "be strong" administrator appears to be rigid and in control at all times. He lives with stress from the effort of holding feelings in abeyance, shows little emotion, and feels uncomfortable when he does express emotions. Because of this apparent inflexibility, this person makes decisions that cause others to lose trust because of lack of communication between the parties. In terms of time management, managers who use this style find themselves spending time clarifying actions they have taken, explaining their decisions, meeting with people to clear up communication conflicts, preparing "clarifying" memoranda, and apologizing to associates for what they have done.

Finally, there is the "please-others-at-all-costs" style of management. This manager's main focus is on making others feel good. This manager accepts others' problems and cannot

---

[6]T. Kahler, and H. Capers. "The Miniscript." *Transactional Analysis Journal* 1974, 4 (1), 26–42.

say "no." In terms of time management, this person tries to please everyone and overextends himself or herself, causing problems for all in planning schedules. At the same time, this person frequently overplans in an attempt to please others or do the right thing.

The healthy-unhealthy cycle illustrated in Figure 1-4, below, represents how we may behave and feel when we become overloaded. Whatever our style is, when we find that we cannot manage our time, the first thing we tend to do is BLAME OTHERS OR THE SITUATION. When this happens, we may look for a scapegoat and say, "I would not have this problem if it were not for the:

> new board policy, or
> students, or
> lousy building, or
> lack of parental support, or
> federal laws, or . . ."

In other words, our initial feeling may be that the cause of the problem is *external* to us.

It is counterproductive to blame others, or the situation, or other external pressures. When we realize that inadequate time management is not totally caused externally, we may enter into the BLAME YOURSELF phase of the cycle. We have all known principals who dwell on their shortcomings or who think they are getting old or who feel time has passed them by. These feelings hurt and are also counterproductive. It is at this stage that serious illness from stress may occur.

As Figure 1-4 illustrates, we suggest two alternatives. First, the problem and symptoms of stress could be ignored with the expectations that they will go away. This could be disastrous, leading to heart attack, hypertension, ulcers, or other stress-related illness. The better route is to take steps to get in control of your job, your stress, your time, and your life.

Figure 1-4

THE HEALTHY-UNHEALTHY CYCLE

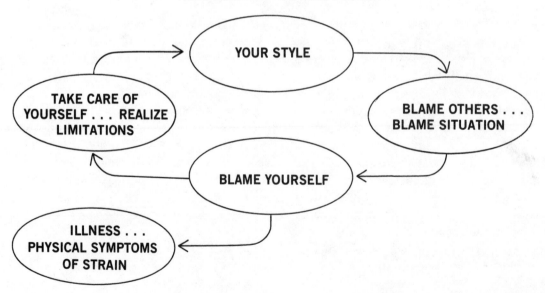

In terms of the styles discussed earlier, the following list describes some things that could be done to overcome the problems inherent in unproductive use of these styles.

If the BE PERFECT style is unproductive for you, try this:

STOP: . . . taking blame for things you cannot influence or control.
. . . worrying about being right.
. . . trying to control everything.
. . . thinking about what others think.
. . . wasting time on things that are not important.
. . . trying to do everything yourself.
START: . . . to let others learn how to do parts of your job.
. . . to allow yourself to make some mistakes.
. . . to think more about long-term goals.
. . . to relax.
. . . to be satisfied that you have done your best.

If the TRY HARDER style is unproductive for you, try this:

STOP: . . . going to work early and leaving late.
. . . taking a full briefcase home each night.
. . . calling or attending night meetings that are not really necessary.
. . . volunteering to do jobs that someone else could do.
START: . . . to take care of yourself.
. . . to say NO!
. . . to work smarter, not harder.
. . . to come to work on time and leave on time.
. . . to realize there is more to life than work.

If the PLEASE OTHERS style is unproductive for you, try this:

STOP: . . . being used.
. . . agreeing to help others at the expense of your own time.
. . . saying yes all the time.
. . . being "the martyr."
. . . signing up for committees or projects that others could do.
. . . always being available.
START: . . . to project the impact on your own time of always saying yes.
. . . to let others do some tasks.
. . . to take care of yourself.
. . . to say no.

If the HURRY UP style is unproductive for you, try this:

STOP: . . . running from place to place.
. . . scheduling meetings back-to-back.
. . . leaving things to the last minute.
. . . trying to do so many things.

START: . . . to plan your own calendar more carefully.
        . . . to anticipate problems and schedule accordingly.
        . . . to delegate.
        . . . to slow down and take care of yourself.

If the BE STRONG style is unproductive for you, try this:

STOP: . . . thinking you are invincible and indispensable.
        . . . worrying about being wrong.
        . . . being concerned about what others think about you.
        . . . feeling you always need to win.
START: . . . to allow yourself to "breathe" more.
        . . . to relax your muscles and built-up tensions.
        . . . to think more of long-term impact of short-term crises.
        . . . to put things into perspective.

CONCLUSION

Now is the time to begin thinking about time management as an approach to improving your leadership skills. Keep the worksheets you copied and completed from this chapter so that you can refer to them as you enhance your administrative style by incorporating the principles of time management.

Periodically review these characteristics of successful managers:

1. The ability to set goals and priorities, and to project into the future.

2. The ability to place activities and issues in order of priority.

3. The ability to delegate to the most qualified staff member or to get others to do tasks to help.

4. The courage to refuse to waste time on the impossible or totally unnecessary tasks.

5. The ability to do it now.

6. The willingness to take time to support, encourage, and show concern for staff and others.

7. The ability to sense time passing.

8. The ability to sense the best time to utilize specific skills.

Chapter **2**

Structuring Your
Time-Management Style

*Putting off an easy thing makes it hard, and putting off a hard one
makes it impossible—George Horace Lorimer*

INTRODUCTION

It is often difficult to structure one's day. There are always fires to be extinguished, teachers and parents wanting to talk to the principal—*only* the principal—and right away. Administrators are constantly being put on system-wide committees, responding to expectations from their central office, and dealing with numerous other unpredictable demands.

Of course, all of these can also be used as rationalizations for not getting to the heart of school administration—instructional leadership. This chapter will help you organize your time so that you may establish plans and procedures that will enable you to work effectively and efficiently with teachers, students, and parents to improve instruction and learning.

PRINCIPLES OF TIME MANAGEMENT

We have identified six principles for effective time management—being aware of self; structuring time appropriately; setting goals and priorities; increasing personal efficiency and effectiveness; setting a time for everything and everything in its time; and scheduling time for physical inactivity. Let us now examine each of these time principles more closely.

1. *Try to develop an awareness of yourself and your job.* A personal awareness must be developed in terms of unique needs, style, characteristics, and management practices. You should examine the job for which you are responsible, and list the main tasks associated with that job. Then you should determine the amount of time you actually use in doing each of those major tasks. This could be achieved in a variety of ways, but leaders in the time-management field usually favor doing this through the use of a time log as discussed in Chapter 1.

Figure 2-1, p. 38, is a worksheet, to be copied and completed in your notebook, that will help analyze your use of time and whether or not you should spend more or less time on a major task. You may feel a task is very important, but when you examine Figure 2-1, discover that you spend no time on it.

Figure 2-1

ANALYSIS OF TIME ON MAJOR TASKS
(complete in notebook)

| MAJOR TASK | AMOUNT OF TIME THAT | | REQUIRED STEPS TO INCREASE OR DECREASE TIME |
	SHOULD BE SPENT	IS SPENT	

Whether you keep a log or use another method to determine what it is you really do, try to establish a specific list of six to eight major categories that represent the ways in which you now use your time. For principals, the list may contain such significant activities as:

a. observing, supervising, and evaluating teachers;

b. meeting with parents and community groups;

c. working with individual pupils and student groups;

d. planning and organizing the curriculum and total school program;

e. handling paperwork, reports, and daily mail;

f. working with support staff such as secretaries, custodians, and aides;

g. working through unexpected demands and crises; and

h. responding to and working with central office personnel.

At any rate, little change or self-improvement will occur without a keen understanding of where and how you use your time.

2. *Structure the way you use time.* Try to structure your time to take into account the important goals of your job. Take, for example, the school secretary who attended a time-management workshop and returned to school all fired up. She immediately made a daily list of what she wished to accomplish the next day. She thought this would help her to accomplish more than ever before. But, within the first half hour of the day, her schedule was shot, and time management was "for the birds." Why?

She simply did not take into account the main functions of her job. She failed to plan for the usual inundation of requests from teachers, the principal, parents, and children during that first half hour. She tried to jump in full force without prior planning. She failed to make contingency plans to deal with daily interruptions. They cannot be willed away. Interruptions will always be there, so a procedure should be developed for dealing with them.

Another important aspect of this principle is that you must adhere to the structure you have established. Quite often we are inclined to avoid the difficult or unpleasant tasks that are on our agenda for a particular day. It is easier to rationalize. The difficult problem will not go away; it must be dealt with. Save yourself some stress and stick to your agenda.

3. *Set goals and daily priorities.* Most of the time-management literature cites goal setting as a common ingredient of successful managers. For school principals, this practice is difficult because of the frequent demands and dependency on school leaders. Teachers, students, parents, and others have come to expect the principal to be available, to have regular contact with them, to be in the halls and classrooms, to listen and respond to questions and concerns, and to be accountable for what goes on in the school. These expectations can cause problems because they can prevent principals from spending time on other essential activities such as setting goals, planning, organizing, or evaluating. Many principals feel it is necessary to expand their workday by coming early and staying late in order to accomplish these activities. It must be recognized that activities like goal setting, planning, setting priorities, and organizing are *integral parts* of the management function, and, as such, should be done during the workday.

The best way to develop and stick to job priorities is to prepare and use a daily "to-do" list as in Figure 2-2, p. 41. Take a few minutes at the close of each day or at the start of each day, close your door, collect your thoughts, and *write down* five tasks you intend to accomplish that day or the next. Make these your priorities for the day. It will help you avoid feelings of frustration and a sense of never accomplishing anything when you can look at that list and actually say, "Well, look at all I accomplished today!" This will be a welcome change from the former time waster saying, "Where does the time go? I just did not get a thing done today."

Priorities must be established so that those tasks dealing with the most important aspect of a job receive the bulk of the time. Indeed, you may have discovered in the analysis of your time log that you are spending the largest percentage of your time on the least important aspects of your job. We believe that if you devote most of your time to the small number of highest priority tasks, you will see a direct increase in effectiveness.

While ranking priorities, you should be looking at whose priorities are ranked highest—your supervisors', the system's, your own, or those of others such as community or pressure groups. In deciding the ranking of each priority, consider whose priority it is, the due date, to whom it is due, and its importance as related to the other functions of your job.

When looking at due dates, try to space out self-imposed deadlines so you will not feel mentally or physically overburdened.

4. *Increase personal efficiency and effectiveness.* All management functions of the school should be reduced as much as possible. The concept of "work simplification" may be used to study the nature of daily routine work and activities. In applying this concept to the management of schools, the principal would study all work done in his office, and in other key operations of the school. The detailed tasks are reviewed for all routine activities, the main goals being to eliminate duplication of effort and reduce time and materials usage. You are attempting to make the job simpler, eliminate waste, and get *maximum* results with *minimum* effort.

In many cases, this way of approaching work is against the cultural expectations or norms. Our society places high value on hard work and the quantity of production rather than the results and quality of the work. This concept is portrayed in Figure 2-3, p. 42. Usually, societal norms require a high score in both columns (10 and 10). Our premise is that we should be attempting to achieve a 10 in quality in conjunction with a 1 in quantity. In other words, work smarter—not harder.

Consider the case of the tough, "hard-nosed" football coach. Coach Tough makes the tackles carry the guards up and down a steep hill. Then, the guards carry the tackles. The coach thinks this is good training. "It makes 'em tough," he explains. In reality, this coach is not "working smart." He should not neglect the development of the skills that tackles and guards need to play their positions; but to dwell too much on meaningless drills is unproductive.

How about the problem one of our friends had with his golf game? He was slicing the ball and thought the solution to this was more practice. After he hit two buckets of balls at a driving range, it became clear that he was not working SMARTER. He practiced HARDER, but still sliced the ball. His slice might be eliminated if he sought advice from a professional golfer who could look at his grip and swing and suggest what the problem could be. Then he could practice SMARTER and *not* compound or perpetuate the problem.

Figure 2-2

EXAMPLES OF DAILY TO-DO LISTS

Example 1

To Do	Priority (A-top, B-medium, C-low)	Why Do It	Due Date	Check One		
				Done	Do Tomorrow	Forget It
1.						
2.						
3.						
4.						
5.						

Example 2

Date	To Do	Check One		
		Done	Do Later	Forget It
	1.			
	2.			
	3.			
	4.			
	5.			

Example 3

To Do (When Done, Cross Off)	Date Done
1.	
2.	
3.	
4.	
5.	

Example 4

Priority Item	Do By	Check When Done
1.		
2.		
3.		
4.		
5.		

Figure 2-3

What Society Expects		
Quality	Quantity
↑ ⑩	⑩ ↑
9	9
8	8
7	7
6	6
5	5
4	4
3	3
2	2
1	1

What We Recommend		
Quality	Quantity
↑ ⑩	10
9	9
8	8
7	7
6	6
5	5
4	4
3	3
2	2
1	① ↓

Managers should also have a clear understanding of the difference between *efficient* and *effective* management. An *effective* manager is concerned about short-term and long-term productivity (results) as well as using efficient means by which that productivity is achieved.

All tasks should be reduced to their simplest form. The inordinate number of routine tasks faced by you in a typical day could be identified by studying your time log. Quite often you will find a routine exists in its present form simply because "we've always done it that way."

Efficiency for many of those routines can be increased by answering the following questions:

1. Is the task necessary?
2. What steps are involved?
3. How many steps are involved?
4. How much time is spent on each task?
5. Can some of the steps be eliminated without negatively affecting quality?
6. Who are the people involved?
7. Can some of the people involved be removed without reducing quality?
8. Can consolidation of tasks or people increase effectiveness and efficiency?

Such a task analysis is extremely important in managing time. Outdated tasks and functions must be examined, and modified, or eliminated if no longer appropriate.

5. *Remember there is a time for everything and everything in its time.* The human animal is prone to avoid unpleasantness, conflict, and difficult chores. The school administrator is included in this description. Frequently, it is extremely difficult to force ourselves into confrontation when we know conflict will result. Forcing ourselves to use conflict-management skills effectively will save many hours otherwise wasted covering for ineffective employees. In addition, when you can comfortably incorporate this principle into your management processes, you will feel much better about yourself in relation to fulfilling your responsibilities.

When people are brought together in a close working relationship, they should expect to have occasions when tension will build to the point of combustion. School administrators must deal with pupil-pupil conflicts, pupil-teacher conflicts, teacher-teacher conflicts, teacher-principal conflicts, teacher-parent conflicts, student-parent conflicts, and even parent-parent conflicts.

Conflict may be negative and, therefore, destructive, or positive and constructive. When conflict is negative, open hostilities often result. Objectivity of the involved parties is no longer in evidence, the self-concept of the individuals moves to the negative side of the scale, and the relationships between the parties deteriorate. One of the distinguishing characteristics of conflict is that it is usually as much an emotional encounter as it is one of issues. Conflict generates feelings that may actually become more important than the issues responsible for the conflict in the first place. It is at this point that the administrator must use conflict-management skills so that the effect on the school is not permanent. The feelings one experiences about and during conflict situations often influence the way in which the conflict is handled.

The recognition of a possible conflict is in itself a positive step toward its resolution. The resolution should prevent or minimize critical situations, and, in fact, become a legitimate part of change. Indeed, the management of conflict does not imply failure, but instead promotes a positive movement toward understanding of differences. It assists in recognizing situations that are potentially critical and developing preventive alternatives. Conflict resolution should clear the air and enhance commitment and, when resolved effectively, it should result in increased creativity.

We have found the following six steps to be effective for conflict resolution. This is not meant to be a comprehensive explanation of conflict management, so we caution you to delve into this area more deeply before attempting resolution of serious conflict.

First, the problem should be defined in terms of both parties' needs. It should be stated so as not to communicate blame or judgment. Each party should state, in his or her own words, the other person's position. Before moving to the second step, be sure both parties accept the definition.

Second, discuss possible solutions, but avoid being evaluative and critical of the solutions suggested. Try, instead, to get a variety of suggestions and then move on to the *third* step of evaluating and testing the solutions suggested in the second step.

Fourth, decide on a solution that is acceptable to both parties.

Fifth, put the agreed-upon solution into practice. Prior to implementation, be sure to decide who does what by when.

Sixth, following implementation, evaluate the solution.

If the conflict could result in personnel action, all steps should be done in writing. In all cases, one should attempt to resolve the conflict after each step.

6. *Schedule time for physical inactivity in completion of long-term goals.* We allow ourselves to become trapped in the "perpetual-motion" syndrome. This syndrome is manifested by the school administrator always being active—busy patrolling halls, busy disciplining, busy composing letters, busy observing teachers, busy conducting and attending meetings, and busy completing forms. Always busy! Always moving! Always visible! It is entirely appropriate and acceptable and necessary to build into your schedule time to think. In order to successfully complete your job, you must plan and keep abreast of current trends and research studies.

Scheduling periods of relative calm between periods that carry with them high levels of stress will also help improve your overall well-being. For example, take a few minutes of "thinking time" to consider *why* particular priorities have been established. Thinking through priorities, problems, or concerns rather than acting on them right away may save valuable time in the long run. Most decisions do not need immediate action, so thinking through them first may save time by having fewer errors and eliminating a need to go through the process a second time.

SEVEN EASY STEPS FOR LONG-TERM PLANNING

It is the responsibility of school administrators to be involved in long-term as well as short-term planning. Both should result in improving the quality of the school. The children who leave that environment should be quite different from those who entered. They must be competitive with students from other schools, they must have salable skills, and they must be socially acceptable. The school administrator has a major responsibility in this and, to insure success, must plan.

We have identified seven steps in the long-term planning process:

1. determining needs
2. establishing goals and objectives
3. collecting data
4. listing the most viable alternatives
5. selecting an approach
6. implementing the plan
7. monitoring and evaluating

Let us briefly examine each step.

1. *Determining needs.* In order to engage in effective long-range planning, you must first determine the needs. What is important? What is not important? How well are particular areas

being attained? We recommend a structured process to gather this information. A model "Needs Assessment" is provided in Figure 2-4, p. 46. Of course, this may be adjusted to reflect concerns unique to your situation.

2. *Establishing goals and objectives.* Once needs are determined through a needs-assessment process, goals and objectives should be established. Goals, based on identified needs, should be set for the long range (3 to 5 years). Objectives can then be developed to help accomplish these goals. These objectives would tend to be short-range in nature. Be sure the goals and objectives are reasonable, and that the objectives are related to the goals.

3. *Collecting data.* Data must be collected throughout the process to help determine how successfully goals and objectives are attained. Pretests should be administered, for example, in a curricular area so it is known where each student begins. Following implementation of the agreed-upon strategy for improvement, posttests should be administered to help determine degree of success.

Data should also be collected to establish the rationale for goals. The goals and objectives must be known and accepted by all members of the staff if the plan is going to have any chance of success. Sometimes the top-level managers of a school system or the board of education do not have clear-cut goals. The school principal, as the middle-level manager, must then press for direction to aid in planning. Some other data sources to help with this could include perceptions of children, parents, and teachers; rate of absenteeism; test score trends; community economic trends; and mobility rates.

To help structure attainment of goals and objectives within a realistic time frame, use the Objectives Time Plan shown in Figure 2-5, p. 50. Remember to relate the objectives to the goals. Select the most important and determine how many can be attained successfully. After the six steps of the Objectives Time Plan have been completed, analyze it and determine how each objective could have been attained more effectively within the same or less time.

4. *Listing the most viable alternatives.* This relates very closely to Step 5, "Selecting an Approach." Input should be obtained primarily from two sources to determine acceptable alternatives. First, call upon available expertise in the field to suggest possible approaches. These people could range from staff within your own building to outside consultants. Second, examine the literature in the field. What does research say? Does what is being done relate positively or negatively to the studies? From these two sources, list the most viable alternatives and then move to Step 5.

5. *Selecting an approach.* After thorough examination and discussion, select the approach that is expected to have the greatest impact. Several questions should be answered here. What are the possible drawbacks to this solution? Are materials required for which there is no money? Are there alternate sources of funding? Is in-service training required? Are those responsible for implementation involved in the planning process? Does this possible solution generate more problems than it solves?

6. *Implementing the plan.* This is the stage where all the planning should show payoffs. If the first five steps have been carefully followed, others should be able to put into action the approach selected in Step 5. It is incumbent upon the administrator to be sure all issues raised in Step 5 are satisfactorily resolved prior to implementation.

Figure 2-4

NEEDS ASSESSMENT

DIRECTIONS: Use the two legends to write in the numeral that best represents your view of the IMPORTANCE and ATTAINMENT of each item. Any item where the ranking of IMPORTANCE is higher than the rating of ATTAINMENT is potentially a "need."

LEGENDS

Ranking of *Importance:*	Rating of *Attainment:*
1. Little Importance	1. Extremely Poor
2. More Importance	2. Poor
3. Medium Importance	3. Fair
4. Major Importance	4. Good
5. Critical Importance	5. Excellent

IMPORTANCE	ITEMS	ATTAINMENT
	I. *Student-Community*	
	a. Student tardiness (decrease of)	
	b. Student attendance (increase of)	
	c. Preparation for enrollment changes (decline or upswing)	
	d. Identification of handicapped and special needs students	
	e. Programs for handicapped and special needs students	
	f. Programs for minority students	
	g. Gifted and talented programs	
	h. Positive student behaviors	
	i. Enrichment programs	
	j. Homework	
	k. Student attitudes toward school	
	l. Counseling programs	
	m. Communication with parents	
	n. School-community relations	
	o. Community involvement in school programs	
	p. School volunteers (quality and sufficient numbers of)	

Figure 2-4 (cont'd)

	I. q. Preparing for changing community characteristics	
	r. Adequacy of the testing program (not scores)	
	s. Other:	

IMPORTANCE	ITEMS	ATTAINMENT
	II. *Administration and Organization*	
	a. Appropriate organizational pattern for instruction	
	b. Articulation between schools	
	c. Transportation program (safe and cost efficient)	
	d. Capacity of school facility	
	e. Quality of school facility	
	f. Maintenance of facility and grounds	
	g. Involvement in budget development process	
	h. Effective and efficient planning	
	i. Effective internal communications	
	j. Other:	
	III. *Personnel*	
	a. Morale of staff (raise)	
	b. In-service participation (increase)	
	c. Quality of in-service	
	d. Effective utilization of aides	
	e. Educational training of staff	
	f. Other:	
	IV. *Program*	
	Systemwide Approaches (use both columns considering appropriateness and quality if now implementing.) (Use only the left-hand column considering the desirability, if not now implementing.)	
	a. Instructional systems: mathematics	
	b. Instructional systems: reading, language arts	

Figure 2-4 (cont'd)

IMPORTANCE	ITEMS	ATTAINMENT
	IV. c. Instructional systems: science	
	d. Instructional systems: social studies	
	e. All-day kindergarten	
	f. Prototype teacher planning	
	g. Science, technology, enrichment program	
	h. Interrelated arts program	
	i. Other:	

IMPORTANCE	ITEMS	ATTAINMENT
	V. *General*	
	a. Adequacy of individualized instruction	
	b. Study skills (improvement of)	
	c. Test-taking skills (improvement of)	
	d. Effectiveness of computer literacy	
	e. Thinking skills (improvement of)	
	f. Internships (quality and increasing number of opportunities)	
	g. Appropriateness and adequacy of team teaching	
	h. Other:	
	VI. *Instructional Approach*	
	a. Quality of instruction and student achievement in ART	
	b. Quality of instruction and student achievement in MATHEMATICS	
	c. Quality of instruction and student achievement in MUSIC	
	d. Quality of instruction and student achievement in PHYSICAL EDUCATION	
	e. Quality of instruction and student achievement in READING/LANGUAGE ARTS	
	f. Quality of instruction and student achievement in SCIENCE	
	g. Quality of instruction and student achievement in SOCIAL STUDIES	

Figure 2-4 (cont'd)

	VI. h. Quality of instruction and student achievement in HANDICAPPED AND OTHER SPECIAL NEEDS	
	i. Quality of instruction and student achievement in EXTRACURRICULAR	
	j. Quality of instruction and student achievement in MEDIA PROGRAM	
	k. Other:	

Adapted from the Montgomery County Public Schools, Maryland.
Permission is granted to reproduce for individual use only.

7. *Monitoring and evaluating.* Stay in touch with those responsible for actual implementation. Are they implementing according to the agreed-upon plan? Are periodic progress meetings scheduled? What additional resources are needed? What changes or modifications are required?

Utilize as many sources as possible in order to properly monitor progress. These sources should include pupils, teachers, and parents. Listen to all viewpoints and perceptions. It might be helpful to ask them to give one strength and one weakness—one thing they like and one they would change. Keep a record of what you hear.

Evaluation should be an ongoing process. Does the plan look as if it is being implemented successfully? Are the objectives being met? Why or why not? What data are used to help determine this? Are the data objective, subjective, or both? What alternatives are being thought of during the process? Finally, should the program be continued as is, should it continue but with modifications, or should it be abandoned?

We recommend the use of hard data as much as possible. Learn to read and interpret achievement test results, both norm-referenced and criterion-referenced. If necessary, take courses in statistics for clarification in using and understanding hard data.

During the monitoring and evaluation stage, do not let your heart work for your brain. Do not be afraid to say we tried and failed. We have to learn from our failures and begin the cycle over. Figure 2-6, p. 51, illustrates the planning cycle.

Figure 2-7, p. 52, provides an example of a long-term curriculum improvement plan developed by a junior high school staff.

Often teachers at one level complain about teachers at the preceding level not covering all of the objectives so that students entering for the new year are not prepared. The new teacher claims that a great deal of time is wasted because he or she must go back and teach what the previous year teacher missed. When a meeting is set up so that these teachers can discuss the curriculum, they seem to have nothing to talk about.

Figure 2-8, p. 55, is designed to help teachers look at their programs and initiate discussion for a smooth transition from one grade level to another.

Figure 2-5

OBJECTIVES TIME PLAN
(complete in notebook)

1. Goal:						
2. Related Objectives	3. Anticipated Methods of Attainment	4. Person Responsible	5. Time Line	6. Evidence(s) of Attainment	7. Date Accomplished	

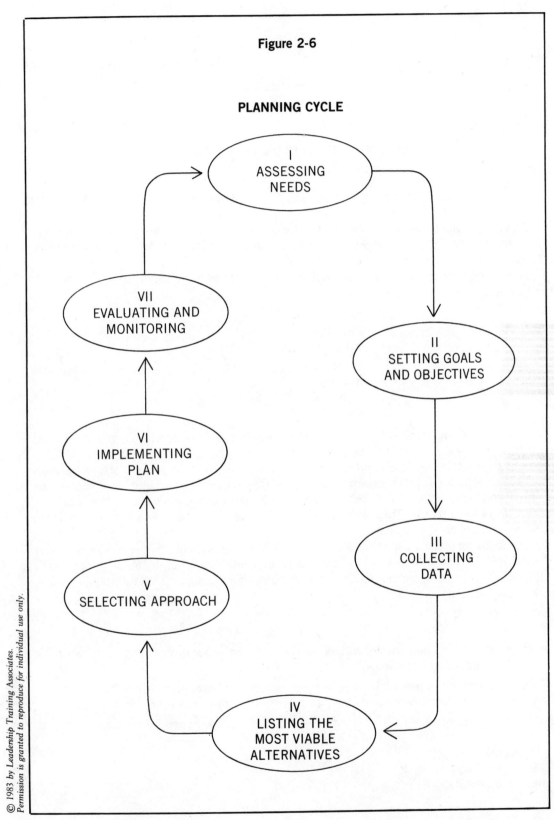

Figure 2-6

PLANNING CYCLE

I
ASSESSING
NEEDS

II
SETTING GOALS
AND OBJECTIVES

III
COLLECTING
DATA

IV
LISTING THE
MOST VIABLE
ALTERNATIVES

V
SELECTING APPROACH

VI
IMPLEMENTING
PLAN

VII
EVALUATING AND
MONITORING

Figure 2-7

Parkland Junior High School
Rockville, Maryland

PLANS FOR CURRICULUM IMPROVEMENT

In the spring of 1979, the total staff adopted the following local school objectives for 1979–80:

All students will experience a coordinated 3-year program in which they learn basic skills in a logical and sequential order. They will apply these skills in a variety of subject areas as part of an integrated program of instruction.

During the summer of 1979, the resource teachers met with the administration to identify the following skills for emphasis:

Reading Comprehension
Math Problem Solving
Writing Skills
Vocabulary
Spelling
Organizational Skills
Listening

The effective achievement of this objective requires a redirection of teaching in most departments. In most cases, this will require a shift away from content-centered instruction toward activities that will teach and reinforce basic learning skills. A proper balance between skills and content instruction is essential. Such a program requires close support and supervision at the departmental level. Resource teachers will need to assume a high level of educational leadership in this process. They, in turn, will need close support and encouragement by the principal and assistant principals.

The following plans are possible means of implementing curriculum improvements related to our objective. It is possible that, for some curriculum changes, a combination of these plans will be most effective. It should be noted that in each plan the departmental resource teacher plays a central role.

Plan A

1. Resource teachers and administrators meet to develop general plans for implementing a specific curriculum improvement.

2. Resource teachers work with total department and/or individual members of the department to identify specific activities and materials regarding the planned curriculum improvement.

3. Individual resource teachers meet with the principal and the appropriate assistant principal to:
   a. report on progress
   b. identify special needs
   c. plan next steps

Figure 2-7 (cont'd)

Plan B

1. Resource teachers, administrators, and specialists meet to develop plans for implementing a specific curriculum improvement.
2. Resource teachers work with total department and/or individual members of the department to identify specific activities and materials regarding the planned curriculum improvement. In this process, they will use the skills and resources provided by the specialist.
3. Individual resource teachers meet with the principal and appropriate assistant principal to:
   a. report on progress
   b. identify special needs
   c. plan next steps

Plan C

1. Resource teachers, administrators, and specialists meet to develop plans for implementing a specific curriculum improvement.
2. Resource teachers coordinate the activities of the specialist with the total department and/or individual department members.
3. The specialist may work to develop new teaching skills within the department or provide direction or resources regarding specific curriculum issues.
4. Individual resource teachers and specialists meet with the principal and appropriate assistant principal to:
   a. report on progress
   b. identify special needs
   c. plan next steps

Plan D

1. The administration and/or specialist meet with the grade level instructional team to develop plans and/or skills for implementing a specific curriculum improvement.
2. Resource teachers coordinate the activities of the specialist with departmental staff and/or work directly with them to identify specific activities and materials regarding the planned curriculum improvement.
3. Individual resource teachers and specialist meet with the principal and appropriate assistant principal to:
   a. report on progress
   b. identify special needs
   c. plan next steps

In support of the above plans, the administration will meet with the total faculty and instructional teams to explain the need for this new process and help to further establish the resource teacher as an educational leader. Area and central office staff will be involved in this process as needed.

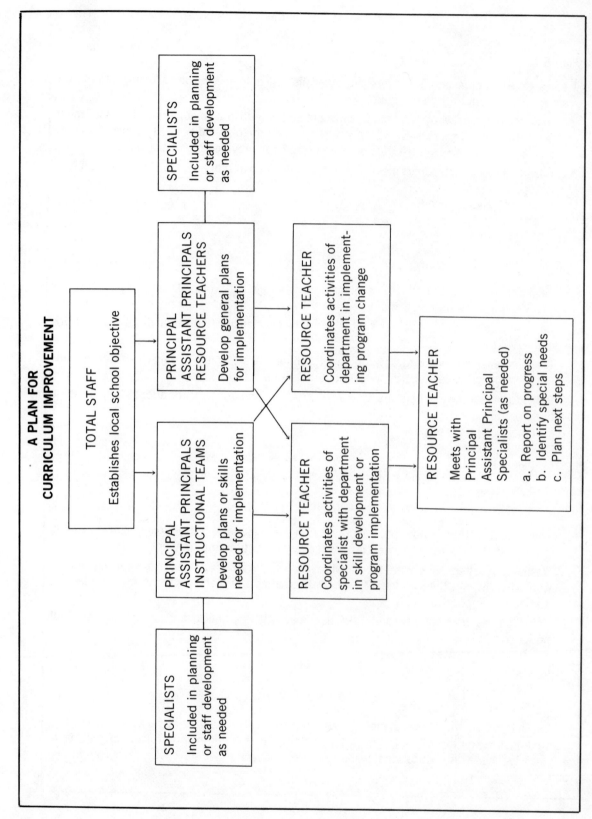

**A PLAN FOR
CURRICULUM IMPROVEMENT**

TOTAL STAFF

Establishes local school objective

SPECIALISTS

Included in planning or staff development as needed

PRINCIPAL
ASSISTANT PRINCIPALS
RESOURCE TEACHERS

Develop general plans for implementation

PRINCIPAL
ASSISTANT PRINCIPALS
INSTRUCTIONAL TEAMS

Develop plans or skills needed for implementation

RESOURCE TEACHER

Coordinates activities of department in implementing program change

RESOURCE TEACHER

Coordinates activities of specialist with department in skill development or program implementation

RESOURCE TEACHER

Meets with
Principal
Assistant Principal
Specialists (as needed)

a. Report on progress
b. Identify special needs
c. Plan next steps

SPECIALISTS

Included in planning or staff development as needed

54

Figure 2-8

ARTICULATION PLAN

I. Receiving Grade or Department
    A. Overview of skills covered at your grade level.
        (1) Language   (5) Spelling
        (2) Math   (6) Science
        (3) Study Skills   (7) Research (as opposed to Study Skills content)
        (4) Map Skills
    B. Expectancy of skills of incoming students that are essential for success at new grade level.
        (1) Language   (5) Spelling
        (2) Math   (6) Science
        (3) Study Skills   (7) Research (as opposed to Study Skills content)
        (4) Map Skills

II. Sending Grade or Department
    A. How does my overview (I-A) coincide or differ from that of receiving grade (I-B)?
        (1) Language   (5) Spelling
        (2) Math   (6) Science
        (3) Study Skills   (7) Research (as opposed to Study Skills content)
        (4) Map Skills
    B. What adjustments have to be made in my organization structure or the organization structure of receiving grade to make for a smooth transition between grade levels?
    C. What dialogue needs to be established, and with whom, to reconcile the differences in order to strengthen the total program for the benefit of the children?
    D. What are the implications for intra-departmental dialogues?

PROCEDURE

The purpose of this exercise is to provide a mechanism whereby teachers may analyze their program in relation to incoming students. The worksheets will help organize thinking so that meaningful dialogue will be facilitated.

1. Every grade level or department reacts to I-A and I-B in that all are "receiving" grade or department.
2. Higher grade level or department gives worksheets I-B to lower grade level or department to look at relationship as outlined in II-A. Keep I-A as guide for deliberations.
3. Each grade level or department writes down questions in II-B.
4. Identify dialogue on paper in II-C.
5. Initiate dialogue to bring about closure.
6. Implement plan from Step 5.
7. Evaluate plan one year later.

NOTE: This should be looked upon as a long-term study, but not to exceed one school year.

ARTICULATION WORKSHEET I-A

Date: _____

School: _____ Grade: _____ Department: _____

_____Language   _____Math   _____Study Skills   _____Map Skills

_____Spelling   _____Science   _____Research   _____Other

Overview of Skills Covered During the Year

(Be concise and general)

1.

2.

3.

4.

5.

6.

7.

8.

9.

10.

11.

12.

ARTICULATION WORKSHEET I-B

Date: _____

School: _____ Grade: _____ Department: _____

_____ Language   _____ Math   _____ Study Skills   _____ Map Skills

_____ Spelling   _____ Science   _____ Research   _____ Other

Skill Expectancy of Incoming Students

(Be concise)

1.

2.

3.

4.

5.

6.

7.

8.

9.

10.

11.

12.

ARTICULATION WORKSHEET II-A

Date: _____

School: _____ Grade: _____ Department: _____

_____Language   _____Math   _____Study Skills   _____Map Skills

_____Spelling   _____Science   _____Research   _____Other

How does my overview I-A coincide with or differ
from that of receiving grade I-B?

Coincide   *Differ*

1.   1.

2.   2.

3.   3.

4.   4.

5.   5.

6.   6.

7.   7.

ARTICULATION WORKSHEET II-B

Date: _____

School: _____ Grade: _____ Department: _____

_____Language   _____Math   _____Study Skills   _____Map Skills

_____Spelling   _____Science   _____Research   _____Other

What adjustments have to be made in my organization structure or the organization of the receiving grade or department to make for a smooth transition between grade levels?

1.

2.

3.

4.

5.

6.

Place an "M" in front of the adjustment number if it is one you should make and an "R" in front of the number if it is one the receiving grade should make.

ARTICULATION WORKSHEET II-C

Date: _____

School: _____ Grade: _____ Department: _____

_____Language   _____Math   _____Study Skills   _____Map Skills

_____Spelling   _____Science   _____Research   _____Other

What dialogue needs to be established, and with whom, to reconcile the differences (II-B) in order to strengthen the program for the benefit of children? Are there implications for other departments?

Dialogue	*With Whom*
1.	1.
2.	2.
3.	3.
4.	4.
5.	5.
6.	6.

SHORT-TERM PLANNING

It is generally true that the higher a person is in the organizational structure, the more he or she should be involved in long-term planning. For example, a superintendent would be involved mostly in this type of planning. Short-term planning should be undertaken by those lower in the organization. The principal, as a middle manager, must be involved from time to time in short-term planning. If this is approached in a logical manner, a great deal of time will be saved by doing away with uncertainties.

Jack had to plan for the sixth grade outdoor education experience that was coming up in seven weeks. The children would be at camp for one week. He used the winter break for his planning session. The first thing he did was to determine what had to be done. His list looked like this:

1. A series of letters to inform parents.
2. Teachers to be given teaching assignments.
3. Student booklet to be made.
4. Materials to be collected.
5. A meeting to inform parents.
6. Survey children for partner selections.
7. Make work group assignments.
8. Make cabin assignments.
9. Make daily schedule.
10. Make weekly schedule.
11. Identify and train patrol substitutes.
12. All materials packed and ready.
13. Order films.
14. Select high school counselors.
15. On-site training.
16. Collect permission slips and money.
17. Depart.

The next step was to set deadlines and meeting dates. The departure date was set for February 6 and it was the end of December when the planning was taking place. This dictated that everything be completed in one month, including who was going to do what. (Delegate.)

Figure 2-9, p. 62, shows the final plan. This type of planning keeps you well organized and saves time that is often lost through poor organization.

CYCLICAL vs. LINEAR PLANNING—WHAT GETS US THERE BETTER

Figure 2-6, p. 51, illustrates the cyclical model of planning and the model we believe to be most effective. Generally speaking, the school year runs from September to June in the

Figure 2-9

HARMONY ELEMENTARY SCHOOL

Calendar of Events for Outdoor Education

Due Date	Activity	By Whom
1/7/81	Letter No. 1 sent home.	Secretary
1/9/81	Teachers to give principal unit numbers planned.	Teachers
1/9/81	Teachers to give principal list of materials needed.	Teachers
1/14/81	Parent Meeting at 7:30 p.m.	Principal
1/16/81	Children to complete typed partner preference sheet. Completed sheets to be given to principal.	Children and Teachers (6th)
1/19/81	Letter No. 2 sent home.	Secretary
1/19/81	Daily and weekly schedules sent to Area Director and Outdoor Education Coordinator.	Secretary
1/23/81	Group and cabin assignments to be completed.	Principal
1/23/81	Student booklet to be ready for typing.	Principal
1/26/81	Letter No. 3 sent home.	Secretary
1/26/81	Meeting at 3:30 p.m. of teachers going to Outdoor Education	Principal
1/29/81	List of children going handed in by teachers— alphabetically by class, boys — girls.	Classroom teachers
1/29/81	5th grade substitute patrols identified and trained.	Mrs. Jones
1/30/81	All material gathered, packed, and ready to go.	Teachers
1/30/81	Student booklet.	Secretaries
1/30/81	Two copies of alphabetical list of students, boys — girls.	Secretary
1/30/81	Teachers new to program and counselors go to Glenkirk for training.	Principal
2/6/81	Depart for camp.	

United States. This creates a sense of "linearity" that should be discouraged and discarded as much as possible. Figure 2-10 illustrates our feeling about linear planning.

For example, we have all heard principals and teachers say, "If I can only get to the winter break . . ." or "Only a few more weeks until the end of school." These comments reflect the linear nature of the educational enterprise. We start everything in September, and we end everything in June. Unfortunately, this mental set causes long-term planning to be neglected. In our recommended *cyclical* planning, we learn from the present to improve the future.

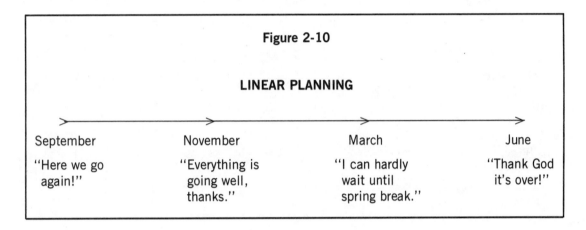

Figure 2-10

LINEAR PLANNING

September	November	March	June
"Here we go again!"	"Everything is going well, thanks."	"I can hardly wait until spring break."	"Thank God it's over!"

CONCLUSION

Instructional leadership should be your primary objective, and the majority of your time must be spent on activities related to this objective.

The following article from *Education, U.S.A.* (January 21, 1980) reinforces this concept.[1]

Schools Can't Be Run from an Office . . .

The key to a good school, according to numerous research studies, is an effective principal who is an "instructional leader." But how many principals are "instructional leaders"? Many attending last week's NASSP meeting admit they or their colleagues are not.

"The trend is toward less and less involvement with curriculum and more paperwork and management responsibilities," said Allan Walker, a past NASSP president. With more required state and federal reports, more special students and more discipline problems, "they plain don't have the time" to be involved in instructional issues, he said.

"The categorical programs have turned the principalship from a leadership position to a bureaucratic one," said NASSP Executive Director Scott Thomson. As research director for NASSP, Thomson headed a study of principals that was released last year. It found a sharp dichotomy between what principals believe their jobs should be and how they were spending most of their time.

---

[1]Reprinted by permission from *Education U.S.A.*, Copyright 1980, National School Public Relations Association.

"As their first priority, they want to be involved in the education program," he said. But they were spending most of their time in management tasks, writing reports, and attending meetings.

What's the answer? Both said some "tough choices" had to be made by top school officials and principals themselves. "Superintendents are going to have to choose either to get some of these reports and responsibilities off principals' backs or to spend more money to get them some help," Walker said. "The education program has suffered because principals are spending all their time in their offices," he said. Thomson agrees that because of a proliferation of responsibilities, "to do the job right, they simply need more help."

But he adds that principals, too, must make some tough choices. "The principal must establish his own agenda," he said. If educational leadership is the top priority, then the principal must see to it that most of his or her time is spent there and that other duties are delegated.[1]

The last paragraph is the key. *Effective Time-Management Techniques for School Administrators* gives many techniques for controlling your own time and organizing activities into a workable schedule. This should provide more time for the instructional components of your job.

---

[1]Reprinted by permission from *Education U.S.A.*, Copyright 1980, National School Public Relations Association.

Chapter 3

How to Make Your Environment Work for You

*A man's time, when well husbanded, is like a cultivated field
of which a few acres produce more of what is useful to life than
extensive provinces even of the richest soil when overrun
with weeds and brambles—David Hume*

INTRODUCTION

Your environment, as discussed in this chapter, is your office. It is here that the major part of your administrative function takes place. Your purpose is to spend less time on administrative duties and more time on the instructional leadership aspects of school administration.

It is very easy to allow yourself to get trapped in this administrivia and become sidetracked. According to Lakein, you must set your A priorities and work toward their completion.[1] These priorities should deal with long-term and short-term instructional goals. By incorporating the suggestions in this chapter and by keeping in mind your A priorities, you will find that you have more time to devote to planning.

SIMPLIFYING WORK THROUGH AN EASY TASK ANALYSIS

If you are going to truly make your environment work for you, you should establish a procedure for simplifying routine tasks. This can be accomplished through structured, simple analysis.

1. Divide the analysis of the task into several steps.
   (a) What is the present procedure?
   (b) Who are the people involved?
   (c) How much time does it take?

---

[1]A. Lakein. *How to Get Control of Your Time and Your Life.* New York: The New American Library, Inc., 1974.

(d) What other tasks should be done during the same time?
(e) What happens to the results?
(f) How long is it in a static state and where?
(g) How much cost is involved?
(h) How many and what kinds of materials must be used?

2. Look for weak spots that are unnecessarily consuming time.
3. Determine changes that could be incorporated to improve the procedure so that it is more effective and less time consuming.

Remember, your purpose is to examine ways of increasing office efficiency. You should be constantly asking yourself, "What will happen if I don't do this task?" or, "How can I make this operation more streamlined and save time and money?" To get the most from your time, you must develop an attitude that everything does not have to be done completely or even at all.

Eighty to eighty-five percent of time should be spent on high-value work. Time expended on low-value items is usually time wasted. Think of work in three phases and try to increase efficiency in all three areas: GET READY — DO IT — PUT IT AWAY. Follow the suggestions in this section and you will find that the length of time will be shortened in performing tasks, but output and quality will be increased. You should be striving to get the best results from the least amount of effort.

HANDLING PAPERWORK THROUGH USING IN BASKETS AND OUT BASKETS

It may not be necessary actually to have a physical container on your desk for incoming correspondence or outgoing responses. Some principals may feel they need those baskets to help them in organizing their routine for handling mail. Other administrators may feel that having the baskets on their desks is distracting, simply takes up space, and provides an excuse for easily overlooking the material. The important thing is what works for you; but to be efficient, there must be a structured process. This efficiency starts with training opportunities for your secretary.

If you do choose an actual in basket/out basket process, we recommend two, or possibly three, baskets. Two trays could be stacked on the corner of your desk within easy reach and could be also easily accessible for your secretary. The bottom one is for incoming mail—the top one for outgoing. You might also want a "wait a week" basket for things you are not sure about. Just wait a week or so. If you don't hear about these things again, shift them to your "round" file.

There are acceptable alternatives to the baskets on the desk model. You could train your secretary to keep three folders: one for the present day's mail, which is scanned quickly for important items; another for items needing your signature, with a set time scheduled weekly for doing that; and a third folder marked "urgent" for "must do" items to help you put things in priority order.

Another suggestion is to work out with your secretary a mutually agreeable mail time. For example, you might agree to report to work a half hour earlier and devote that time to the mail. It can be gone through together. Some can be handled routinely by the secretary, which will save you time as long as you are at least kept informed. On other pieces of mail you can write an action to be performed or the name of an appropriate person to whom action can be delegated. Other responses may require immediate dictation to your secretary. In any event, whatever mail is not completed within that half hour is held until the next day and placed on top of the next day's mail.

Several other suggestions could be incorporated into your own style. Have your secretary sort all mail before it comes to you—important items on the top and less important on bottom. After it is sorted and transferred to you, do something with each piece of paper.

Set aside a regular time each day for paperwork. We recommend no more than 30 minutes daily as a basis. All paper items should be ordered by importance, and 80 percent of the time should be spent on high-priority items. Spend short periods of time doing something—some little task—that moves the high-priority items ahead.

If you feel it is necessary to read flyers, catalogs, and routine articles, save them to be read once a week. Have your name removed from mailing lists that provide you with junk mail. Ask others to let you know about new ideas and materials. Unless you're superhuman, you cannot do everything yourself.

Ask yourself what will happen if the letter or memo is not answered. If you're not sure, it might be a good one for the "wait a week" basket. If you do need to respond, write responses directly on the letter or memo. If you believe nothing will happen by not responding, throw it away. Learn to be comfortable with throwing out more papers. Do not save everything; but if you cannot bring yourself to throw them away, at least ask others to save them for a later date. (You will probably forget them.)

PHYSICAL ARRANGEMENT OF OFFICE MAKES "COMFORTABLE EFFICIENCY"

The physical arrangement of the office area should promote contact with pupils, parents, and staff, but must allow for efficient office operation. Your own office should be neat, pleasant, and conducive to informal meetings, as well as a place for business and formal activities such as staff evaluation or difficult disciplinary actions. Remove all items that are unnecessary or take up too much space in your office. Do not make your office too comfortable so that people are encouraged to stay longer than needed; for example, chairs should be straight and not too plush. Conference-type furniture should be away from your desk. Professional books and curriculum guides should be on shelves in your office but not necessarily within arm's reach, unless used frequently. Have a bulletin board within eyesight containing important or frequently used schedules or announcements.

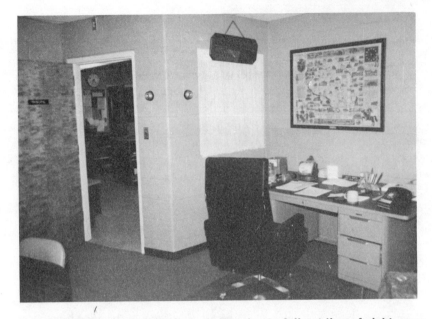

By positioning your desk facing a wall and out of direct line-of-sight, you avoid a great many eye contact distractions.

Secretaries must be able to have privacy to do their work, but they must also be able to act as receptionists. Locate your secretary's desk physically so that she can act as a buffer to anyone who may want to interrupt you. This way she can screen the visitors, perhaps handle many of the responses herself, direct them to others who can adequately respond, or schedule an appointment with you, if necessary.

Locate your desk so that it is not visible from the outer office. This eliminates casual greetings and a great deal of wasted time.

Review the efficiency of your operation periodically and change to a new or different one. Throw out materials not used. Keep only the useful material. Think: "How can I make this office more efficient and still keep it comfortable?"

ORGANIZING YOUR DESK SO IT HELPS YOU SAVE TIME

The "stacked desk syndrome"[2] simply allows one to say to oneself, "Look how busy I am," and then becomes a security blanket. Also think about how easy (or convenient?) it is to lose an important paper on a cluttered desk. What a time waster that can be!

I used to tell my secretary not to put the papers on my desk in order because I knew where everything was and could find it immediately. After I missed some deadlines and I lost some important papers, I did away with the "stacked desk syndrome."

Your desk should be clear with only necessary and frequently used items on it and in it. Train, and give the authority to, your secretary to keep it clear. If you are an administrator who decides to use the in basket/out basket containers, stack them on top of one another for efficiency. If you don't use baskets, still keep one place on your desk for incoming material and another place for material to be distributed.

Have all needed materials within reach so you do not constantly have to get up to get them. Such distractions will prevent you from getting deeply involved in a priority task. Examples of items to have readily available could be pens, pencils, paper, employee personnel folders, school system policies and procedures, and copies of the union contracts.

---

[2]R. Rowan. "Keeping the Clock From Running Out."

Your desk should be orderly so that you can immediately find needed papers. Often-used files and confidential records should also be readily accessible.

Books that are referred to frequently should be on the shelf closest to you. The most important and often-used folders should be in a desk drawer file. Another desk drawer should be well stocked with "hardware"—paper clips, scissors, staples, stapler, and other similar items needed for efficient operation. Another drawer should be reserved for personal items—hairbrush, toothbrush, medication, tissues, etc.

Your telephone should be in an unobtrusive place such as the corner of the desk or a small nearby table. Important and the most often-used phone numbers should be listed in alphabetical order on a pad kept beside the telephone.

Of course, since our goal is to have you better manage your time, your appointment calendar is an important asset that should be kept on your desk within easy reach.

FILING SYSTEMS—TO FILE OR NOT TO FILE

An efficient filing system enables the retrieval of items needed on a moment's notice. Many systems can achieve this, but whatever system is used should be clearly understood by both you and your secretary. In fact, your secretary should take care of most filing.

Files should promote more efficient operating procedures. A few personal, confidential, and frequently used folders may be kept in your own desk or office, but most should definitely be kept in the general office.

All folders should be kept in alphabetical order and filing cabinet drawers labeled according to function. Files should be cleaned out regularly with items being discarded when they are not active or are not likely to be needed in the future. DO NOT HORDE USELESS MEMORANDA!

This is one method of dealing with "junk mail" which does not move you toward completion of your major objective.

The filing cabinets should be in a file room or an unobtrusive corner in order to be readily accessible but not in the way. If you have a lot of file material, make sure there is a method to keep track of files removed from a cabinet. For example, a card could be inserted in the place of a file folder that is removed or a log could be kept of who removed the folder, when it was removed, and when it was returned.

HOW TO MANAGE DAILY ROUTINES AND STILL KEEP THEM ROUTINE

If managing daily routines has become a major time consumer of yours, it is probably because you (1) lack priorities, (2) maintain too much control over subordinates, (3) refuse to delegate, or (4) feel more secure when dealing with details of daily operations.

Routine trivia and items of low value that do not move you toward completion of your major objectives should be minimized, consolidated, delegated, or eliminated as much as possible. Principals should separate themselves from unnecessary detail and selectively neglect all but essential tasks. Some would consider managing of routine trivia a major time waster.

You must set and concentrate on goals. Do not hesitate to delegate nonessential activities; and when you have done so, give those to whom you have delegated plenty of time and freedom to reach the objective. Keep your eye on results, not the details of those results. Recognize that without delegation, it is nearly impossible to get everything done.

For those daily routines that cannot be handled in any way except by doing them yourself, prepare a daily "to do" list, establish priorities, and then do them in that order; do not procrastinate. Try to establish a set time to do routine tasks each day—paperwork, telephone calls, daily schedules, reviewing materials, and thinking. Try to do routines in a quiet time of the day so you will not be distracted. Keeping to such a routine takes perseverance and focused attention.

You know better than anyone else the time in the day or during the year when you will be most or least disrupted by pupils, teachers, or parents. Build your routine accordingly. Anticipate peak and low times of activity. Do not even try to do an important report or memo when you know it is likely that you will be interrupted.

A great deal of time may be made available for higher priority items by establishing routines for daily chores. It is extremely important that you and your secretary operate on the same wavelength. Have your secretary answer the questions in Figure 3-1, p. 73, while you fill out Figure 3-2, p. 75. (Keep answers on notebook paper in your notebook.) When you have finished, compare answers. This is a valuable tool for the development of efficient office management.

HOW TO STOP PAPERWORK FROM BREAKING YOUR BACK

If allowed, paperwork can be one of the school administrator's most time-consuming activities. It is tempting to show one's indispensability by keeping a large stack of paper on the desk. This also adds to the strong possibility of wasting time by having to search for an important document that has been lost among other papers.

Mackenzie says the most common cause of paperwork frustration is indecision. He says the average administrator should be able to make an immediate decision on about 80 percent of the items in the in basket.[3] Again, the key here seems to be to delegate.

He goes on to say that Ralph Cordiner, former Chairman of General Electric, always kept his desk clear in order to guarantee that he would have no more than one important matter in front of him at a time.

If you prefer not to scan your mail as suggested earlier, then we suggest you try never to move a piece of paper over your desk more than once. On a memo directed to you, reroute by writing a note on it to the appropriate staff member for review or action. Again, try to do the paperwork at a set time each day. For example, a half hour of quiet time at the beginning of the day as referred to earlier, or the end of the day when staff and students are gone might help send you home with a feeling of having accomplished much.

In setting priorities, spend time on paperwork according to those priorities. Do not become a slave to the paperwork. Only spend the amount of time necessary to move toward major goals. Do not use the paperwork as an excuse to avoid more important tasks even though they may be more difficult. Do the most important paperwork first and either discard unimportant paperwork, or spend a minimal amount of time on it.

Work closely with your secretary and have her develop memoranda, short letters, and other responses or materials whenever possible, or draft responses and let your secretary do the writing from your draft. You can select or train your secretary to check your work for the mechanics of written expression.

Write some responses directly on the incoming letter or memo; this will save both time and paper. When you write letters or memos, keep them short and to the point. Do not try to be a perfectionist. Do not waste valuable time trying to impress others. Do your best, but do not

---

[3]R. Mackenzie. *The Time Trap.*

Figure 3-1

Secretary Questionnaire

Do You

Yes	No	Would Like	
			TELEPHONE
			1. Place outgoing calls for your principal?
			2. Handle parental complaints?
			3. Deal with requests for information?
			4. Make decisions as to which calls are important and which can be handled by someone else?
			5. Answer the phone in a pleasant voice?
			6. Use good human relation skills when dealing with a complaint?
			CORRESPONDENCE
			7. Screen all notes leaving the principal's office?
			8. Respond to some requests using your signature?
			9. Compose some letters from notes?
			10. Anticipate a response and initiate a letter?
			11. Make corrections on language usage, spelling, organization, etc.?
			12. Do your own proofreading accurately?
			13. Read all incoming mail so that you are informed?
			14. Route incoming mail to the proper person?
			15. Remove all junk mail?
			16. Place incoming mail in the "in" basket, in accordance with the schedule for handling?
			17. Remove correspondence from the "out" basket on a regular schedule?
			18. Summarize lengthy reports or letters?
			FILES
			19. Have a filing system that is designed for easy retrieval and that your principal can use in your absence?
			20. Keep up-to-date on your filing?
			21. Have a check-out system for files that are removed?
			22. Maintain a "confidential" file in a locked file drawer in the principal's office?
			23. Maintain a tickler file for future-action items?
			24. Maintain a monthly schedule of routines that happen at the same time, yearly?

			Figure 3-1 (cont'd)
Yes	No	Would Like	
			MEETINGS
			25. Notify those involved in advance?
			26. Help gather materials and prepare visuals?
			27. Make sure space is available?
			28. Make sure all necessary equipment is in place?
			29. Keep minutes of all meetings?
			SCHEDULING APPOINTMENTS
			30. Keep a calendar of the principal's schedule?
			31. Update the calendar daily (reconcile the desk calendar with the personal calendar carried in pocket or purse)?
			32. Make appointments with proper time allocations? (Appointments should not be open-ended)
			33. Avoid scheduling an appointment when the person should be seeing someone else?
			34. Interrupt when time has expired?
			VISITORS
			35. Make visitors feel welcome and comfortable?
			36. Give new students and parents a warm feeling for the school?
			37. Help visitors and teachers when possible without bothering the principal?
			38. Act as a buffer to intercept drop-in visitors?
			MISCELLANEOUS
			39. Keep a folder of all pertinent information for a substitute?
			40. Help in training new employees?
			41. Demonstrate punctuality, loyalty, and conscientiousness?
			42. Know where your principal is and when he or she is expected back?
			43. Meet with your principal each day to have questions answered and set priorities?
			44. Keep aware of deadlines and inform the principal of the status in relation to deadlines?
			45. Maintain confidentiality?
			46. Receive support from your principal?

			Figure 3-2
			Principal Questionnaire
			Does Your Secretary

Yes	No	Would Like	TELEPHONE
			1. Place outgoing calls for you?
			2. Handle parental complaints?
			3. Deal with requests for information?
			4. Make decisions as to which calls are important and which can be handled by someone else?
			5. Answer the phone in a pleasant voice?
			6. Use good human relation skills when dealing with a complaint?

			CORRESPONDENCE
			7. Screen all notes leaving your office?
			8. Respond to some requests using his or her own signature?
			9. Compose some letters from notes?
			10. Anticipate a response and initiate a letter?
			11. Make corrections on language usage, spelling, organization, etc.?
			12. Do his or her own proofreading?
			13. Read all incoming mail so that he or she is informed?
			14. Route incoming mail to the proper person?
			15. Remove all junk mail?
			16. Place incoming mail in the "in" basket, in accordance with the schedule for handling?
			17. Remove correspondence from the "out" basket on a regular schedule?
			18. Summarize lengthy reports or letters?

			FILES
			19. Have a filing system that is designed for easy retrieval and that you can use in his or her absence?
			20. Keep up-to-date on his or her filing?
			21. Have a check-out system for files that are removed?
			22. Maintain a "confidential" file in a locked file drawer in your office?
			23. Maintain a tickler file for future-action items?
			24. Maintain a monthly schedule of routines that happen at the same time every year?

Figure 3-2 (cont'd)

Yes	No	Would Like	MEETINGS
			25. Notify those involved in advance?
			26. Help gather materials and prepare visuals?
			27. Make sure space is available?
			28. Make sure all necessary equipment is in place?
			29. Keep minutes of all meetings?
			SCHEDULING APPOINTMENTS
			30. Keep a calendar of your schedule?
			31. Update the calendar daily (reconcile the desk calendar with your personal calendar)?
			32. Make appointments with the proper time allocations? (Appointments should not be open-ended.)
			33. Avoid scheduling an appointment when the person should see someone else?
			34. Interrupt when time has expired?
			VISITORS
			35. Make visitors feel welcome and comfortable?
			36. Give new students and parents a warm feeling for the school?
			37. Help visitors and teachers when possible without bothering you?
			38. Act as a buffer to intercept drop-in visitors?
			MISCELLANEOUS
			39. Keep a folder of all pertinent information for a substitute?
			40. Help in training new employees?
			41. Demonstrate punctuality, loyalty, and conscientiousness?
			42. Know where you are and when you are expected back?
			43. Meet with you each day to have questions answered and set priorities?
			44. Keep aware of deadlines and inform you of the status in relation to deadlines?
			45. Maintain confidentiality?
			46. Receive support from you?

overdo. Write some notes or memos by hand. A handwritten note is sometimes better received than a formal letter.

Obtain and use paper of different sizes—3″ × 3″ for short notes, 5″ × 8″ for other material, and 8½″ × 11″ for longer letters or memoranda. Make only the number of copies needed and have them distributed to those who need them. Remember, others are busy, so don't add to their paper overload. Do not become an adherent of what Rowan referred to as the Fat Paper Philosophy, induced by memoitis and spread by copying machines.[4]

WHEN AND HOW TO USE THE TELEPHONE SO IT DOES NOT CONTROL YOUR LIFE

Based on experience of managers in 15 countries, Mackenzie ranked telephone interruption as the Number 1 time waster.[5] Leo B. Moore of the Massachusetts Institute of Technology worked with almost 3,000 managers in executive development programs in a study done over a period of six years and also concluded that the telephone was the Number 1 time waster.

Problems with telephones center around the frequency and length of calls. Do not let the phone rule your life. It is a tool that should be there to help you. If you are involved and the phone rings and no one else is available to answer it, let it ring! If it is important, the caller will call back.

You do not have to interrupt your work to answer the phone or to talk immediately with all callers.

Are all calls to you or made by you business related? We suggest you keep a time log of phone calls for one week for analysis. (See Figures 3-3 and 3-4, p. 78.)

---

[4]R. Rowan. "Keeping the Clock From Running Out."
[5]R. Mackenzie. *The Time Trap.*

Figure 3-3

(Keep in your notebook)

Time Log (Telephone) Date: __4/30__

	Beginning Time	Originator	Purpose	Ending Time	Total Time
1.	7:03 a.m.	me	set appointment with boss	7:06 a.m.	3 min.
2.					
3.					
4.					
5.					

Figure 3-4

(Keep in your notebook)

Time Analysis (Telephone) Date: __4/30__

Call Number	Could it have been handled by someone else?		If yes, who?
	Yes	No	
1.	√		secretary
2.			
3.			
4.			
5.			

The analysis should include who placed the call, its purpose, the length of time of the conversation, and whether it could have been handled by another person. From this analysis you should be able to make some generalizations to help modify procedures. For example, you may notice that many of your calls are simple inquiries for which you had to seek out information and then return the calls when, in all probability, your secretary could have taken care of them.

Never accept being put on hold. Depending upon the priority of the call, either leave a message to have the call returned or say you'll return the call. We have all had the experience of being put on hold and forgotten. Of course, if your desk is organized efficiently and a paperwork routine has been established, it is possible that you could be doing paperwork if you do choose to wait on hold.

While you are on the phone, stay with the task at hand. Small talk with everyone who calls is a great time waster. You don't have to be brusque or rude, just say, "I have a teacher with whom I must talk. Could I call you back when we both have more time to chat?" For those callers who, you know from past experience, tend to be windy, you could start the conversation by saying, "I thought I'd get to you now while I have a few unscheduled minutes," or you can have your secretary primed to interrupt you with another "appointment." If you really get desperate, you can hang up in the middle of the conversation while *you* are talking as if you have been cut off.

Have some phrases established in your mind for gracefully, but firmly, ending calls. For example, "Bruce, I'd like to talk more, but I have an appointment shortly for which I must prepare," or "Mary, before we hang up . . .," or "Bob, I've enjoyed talking with you . . ."

You do not have to interrupt your work to answer the phone or to talk immediately with all callers. As much as possible, train and rely on others to screen incoming calls and take messages for those that must be directly handled by you. If trained properly, the person initially taking the calls can manage most of those that turn out to be routine. You may want to shut down the telephone for one hour each morning, allowing someone else to take messages during that period rather than put through any incoming calls.

Another time organizer is setting a specific time each day to return phone messages. The last half hour of each day may be routinely set aside to do this or use 11:30 a.m. People are frequently getting ready to go to lunch or to go home at those times and do not want to get involved in social chitchat so they will stick to the purpose of the call.

Make a priority list of calls. Have a three-minute timer placed beside the phone and try to limit your calls this way. If possible, return all phone messages on the same day they are received. If a call has some complexity—it is long distance or the number must be looked up—have your secretary do it. If you do not get an answer, have your secretary take over. Do not waste time on repeated attempts to a busy or unanswered line. Any time that remains could be used as a quiet time for reading, meditating, or working on your Number 1 priority.

For calls that may be lengthy, organize yourself before calling. Prepare a specific list of those items you wish to cover, stick to that list, and check off the items as discussed. Be prepared to respond to anticipated questions. Do not waste valuable time (yours or the caller's) by going on hold while seeking an answer.

Rather than writing memos or letters, consider solving problems by using the phone. A conference call could be more efficient. You could rent or purchase a conference call attachment to enable others to participate in telephone meetings.

An answering service attachment could also be rented or purchased. Used correctly, such a device could save valuable time and would be especially helpful in schools having no one but the principal available to answer the phone.

HOW TO ORGANIZE YOUR CALENDAR SO IT BECOMES YOUR BEST FRIEND

Organize your calendar at the beginning of each school year. First, place on it the meeting dates established by your school district. For example, the superintendent meets with all administrative staff on the mornings of the third Wednesday of each month or the instructional supervisors meet with principals at 9:00 a.m. every other Thursday. Next, put in all holidays. Third, enter regular meetings you will probably schedule with your own staff including times for total staff meetings as well as times with smaller groups such as grade level teams or department chairpersons. (See Chapter 7.) Fourth, put in observations of staff for whom you have responsibility (See Chapter 6.)

Your calendar should be one that is sectioned into blocks of time—15 minutes, half hours, or hours at most. (See Figure 3-5, p. 81.) Have your secretary make appointments, place them and other important functions on the calendar, and keep the calendar current. If you prefer not to keep the calendar visible on your desk, have your secretary give you a daily agenda or meeting schedule on a 3″ × 5″ card. Any information that may be required for an appointment should be ready ahead of time. This makes it incumbent upon the person who makes the appointment to determine the purpose so that needed information can be readied.

Do not allow the entire day to be blocked out for appointments. Remember that most people who want to be on your calendar also keep a calendar. Therefore, they will probably understand if you are unable to arrange an appointment with them on the first try. Do not overschedule or backlog your meetings too closely. Nobody likes to be kept waiting when specifically scheduled for an appointment. You are better off underscheduling than overbooking and then being embarrassed when you cannot keep an appointment.

Do not run yourself ragged by scheduling things on top of each other. Anticipate the unexpected demands that may occur on certain days, weeks, or months. For example, it would be poor planning to schedule an important conference from 2:00 p.m. to 3:00 p.m. on the day before a vacation begins.

Leave some blank time to accommodate unexpected interruptions. Build in times for planning and doing lengthy tasks. Block in your times for your "to do" list.

If you have an appointment in someone else's office or work location, arrange to arrive as closely as possible to the agreed-upon time. Arriving five, ten, or more minutes early can be wasted time. It would be wise to carry with you something that can be done if you are early or if the other person is not an efficient time manager and forces you to wait. You could have your signature folder with you, a memo or report that needs to be read, or some correspondence that needs answering. Of course, you could also use this time wisely by preparing last-minute thoughts before the upcoming meeting.

Be sure to build in time for lunch, rest, and relaxation. Research supports this notion. A person's error rate increases with lack of rest. Working while eating lunch or skipping lunch altogether may, in actuality, be wasting time since more time may have to be spent correcting errors made due to lack of rest.

Figure 3-5

SEPTEMBER
16
Thursday

	September 1980					
S	M	T	W	T	F	S
		1		2	3	4
5	6	7	8	9	10	11
12	13	14	15	16	17	18
19	20	21	22	23	24	25
26	27	28	29	30	31	

8 30 } Austin – obs.

9 30 } class visits
}

10 30 } aide schedules
–10:30 Miller

11 30 }
} mail

12 30

1 30 } newsletter

2 30
Phone: 555-1278
–2:45 Mrs. Person – re: Testing Jim for learning disability
(Poor reader but good in other areas)

3 30 } ESAA

4 30 –4:00 – 4:45 Early Admission Meeting
Room 240 – diagonally across from Dr. Sterns' office
Program Development

5 30

EVENING APPOINTMENTS AND MEMOS

USING A TAPE RECORDER OR DICTAPHONE—
WHAT DO YOU MEAN, I TALK TOO MUCH?

The use of a tape recorder or dictaphone could be a time saver for both you and your secretary. You can dictate into a recording device when the ideas are fresh as well as when it is convenient for you. In the same way, your secretary can transcribe when it is convenient for her, thus, helping her manage her time effectively. Using a dictating machine will prevent time from being wasted while waiting for your secretary to become available to gather pad and pen, and to come to your office. We even advise you to carry a tape recorder in your car.

In a survey by Howard it was shown that 40 percent of the executives surveyed write memos and letters to be typed.[6] In *The Time Trap*, Mackenzie writes that the pace of handwriting is 20 to 30 words per minute as compared to 150 words per minute that can be spoken.[7] In addition, one can speak two times faster than shorthand can be taken. At this rate, one hour using dictating equipment equals five hours of handwriting time or four hours giving and taking dictation. MacKenzie also points to a study by the U.S. Navy that material can be transcribed from a machine 33 percent faster than from longhand or shorthand. CAUTION! Using a dictaphone or tape recorder could become so easy and you could become so verbose that you end up wasting a lot of people's time rather than saving it.

In discussing your environment, we have frequently mentioned your secretary. You undoubtedly realize that we feel this position is vitally important to a successful school operation. In Chapter 4 we will go into more detail about using your secretary as a time saver.

We are aware that in some jurisdictions, the principal may not be provided with a secretary. If this is the case in your district, you might approach the Board of Education for additional appropriations to provide some degree of secretarial support. This relatively small expenditure would pay vast dividends to the children by freeing you, a trained professional, from performing secretarial functions and enabling you to devote more time to curriculum development.

WORKING WITHOUT A SECRETARY SURE DOES TAKE TIME

If the parents realize that you are the instructional leader and your presence observing can initiate change, they will be glad to volunteer and help in the office. The help parents can give you will allow you time to train and in-service your volunteers about all aspects of a school. Try to find parents who can type, but beggars can't be choosers, therefore take any volunteer with whom you feel you can work. If parent volunteers are not what you want then try retired senior citizens. A federally funded program under the Action Division called RSVP (Retired Senior Volunteer Program) has a coordinator in every state. Contact that person and go from there. The retired person is a great untapped resource we do not use. Remember that people like those for whom you have worked, and whom you greatly respected, will retire, or have retired—use them. It fulfills a need we all have of being needed and it helps fill your needs of running an efficient office and school.

---

[6]D. Howard. "Executive Workload—The Triumph of Trivia." *The Wall Street Journal*, August 13, 1968.
[7]R. Mackenzie. *The Time Trap.*

Other ways to obtain help to relieve you of details and free your time for instruction are: vocational-technical students, other high school students, business school students, and college volunteers.

The use of some of your students for answering the telephone at different times is helpful. This is not taking advantage of your students, but with a little training can be a learning experience for them. Proper telephone techniques, politeness, essentials of taking a complete telephone message (date, time, who called, and will they call back or do they want you to return the call) are all good lessons for students to learn.

CONCLUSION

The administrivia that confronts us daily is too often the "tail that wags the dog." We must not let minuscule routines control our lives. The ideas and techniques discussed in this chapter reduce time spent on low-priority items to 20 percent, and help us to devote 80 percent of our time to high-priority tasks.

Chapter 4

What to Do About Overload

*We always have time enough, if we will but
use it aright—Johann Wolfgang von Goethe*

INTRODUCTION

By now, you may have come to the conclusion that nothing goes as planned in school administration. You walk out of your office with a definite purpose in mind and before you get five steps away you are confronted by ten problems that cause you to promptly forget the reason for leaving your office. If this is the case, you might be suffering from a bad case of overload. This chapter will help you to recognize when you are suffering from overload and how to do something about it.

HOW TO HAVE AN OPEN-DOOR POLICY THAT DOES NOT TAKE TOO MUCH TIME

This idea started with Marco Polo and China—which goes to show how long a bad idea can last. An open-door policy is one that many educators would say is the first principle of good human relations and public relations programs, but it is also one of the greatest time wasters. Unfortunately, you may have been taught the importance of being available to *all people* who need you *whenever* they need you. To a certain degree, this is true; but a complete open-door policy is not needed. What is needed is an open-door philosophy and attitude, but one with guaranteed structure. An efficient time manager can practice the principles of an open-door policy and still not have it interfere with good time utilization.

We suggest you structure your open-door policy through use of several techniques.

• Plan your unavailability. Close the door to do work that requires strict concentration. Be sure your secretary and others know the closed door means you are working on an important project or task that requires your close, personal attention and you should not be interrupted. The closed door also reinforces your secretary when she tells people you are busy and cannot be interrupted.

• Set aside a quiet hour each day and always have the door closed during this time. Get people accustomed to it and let only dire emergencies interfere. People will hesitate to open or knock on a closed door. One quiet hour per day will enable you to get much more accomplished than eight hours with interruptions and distractions that come with an open door.

• Leave your door ajar when you may be interrupted. People will think twice before pushing it open. This can be done when you are working on less important mail or matters to which you may easily return after an interruption. This communicates to teachers and other staff, "It is okay to come in. I am working on something easily interrupted." At the same time, this will enable staff to reach the point where they will stop and say to themselves, "Is this really so important that I must see the boss right now?" Chances are strong that if it can wait, solutions will be thought of without involving the boss.

• Find a hideaway somewhere in the building where there is little traffic and it is peaceful. Unless you are a very unusual person, it is not possible to concentrate fully without some seclusion from noise and distraction. If people come to your office and see it empty, they will generally not go looking for you somewhere else.

Does all this mean you should cease to be available and accessible to staff, children, and parents? Of course not. But it does mean you do not sit in the office with the door open all day waiting. There are other tasks that must be done.

Plan your time so that you are available during specific periods to see teachers—periods when they are free from teaching responsibilities. If the teaching day is from 9:00 a.m. to 3:00 p.m. and teachers work from 8:30 a.m. to 4:00 p.m., then 8:30 a.m. to 9:00 a.m. and 3:00 p.m. to 4:00 p.m. should be reserved solely for teachers. Times to see parents and students can be more flexible.

You can post a calendar blocking out times when you are available to teachers. Allow teachers to schedule their own times to see you, but require that the scheduling be completed by 9:00 a.m. so you are able to plan the rest of your day. If you do not set an arbitrary time by which an appointment must be scheduled, you may create human relations problems. For example, someone signs up at 10:00 a.m. (an hour past the deadline) for an appointment at 10:30. You have checked the schedule shortly after the 9:00 a.m. deadline and determined that you will be free until 11:30 a.m. so you go to talk with the secretary or business manager about setting up a new bookkeeping procedure. During this time period you have missed a 10:30 appointment that you did not even know you had. The teacher was sure she had an appointment with you. As far as she is concerned, you are unavailable and inaccessible because a prearranged deadline was either not followed or not set.

In summary, an open-door policy is good as long as *you* remain in control. Do not let a door control your life.

PLAN AHEAD FOR UNEXPECTED INTERRUPTIONS

Research data indicate that school administrators' activities are so frequently interrupted that the administrators have little opportunity to devote total attention to a single task. Does this mean we simply give up and try to get by with minimal efficiency and effectiveness? Or does it mean more attention needs to be paid to our use of effective time-management techniques?

Since unexpected interruptions will occur, *plan ahead* to be ready to cope with as many of these interruptions as possible. Make a list of all the interruptions that you can anticipate happening. Look at the list and group the items into categories.

One category could include those unexpected interruptions that require immediate attention and, most likely, assistance from an outside agency, such as fire or police. Another might include those interruptions that require immediate attention but no assistance from an outside agency, such as a minor injury. A third category can be those items that could be deferred, such as phone calls.

Now establish procedures for handling, at the minimum, the broad categories and, whenever possible, specific instances. This is contingency planning. We fully realize that every interruption cannot be planned for ahead of time; but we hope that the majority of the interruptions will fit into one of the broad categories.

Be sure to decide who would make decisions for emergency actions when the principal is not in the building.

DROPPING OUT DROP-IN VISITORS

Most school administrators have been indoctrinated into believing that they must be available to everyone at all times. They drop whatever they are doing to respond to telephone requests or to talk with anyone who drops in to chat. Visitors come unannounced and expect the administrator to respond to their demands or requests immediately. While it is important to be available to help, we feel that sometimes school administrators suffer from "overreact-itis." One must learn to handle drop-in visitors graciously but with a very strict awareness of the time that is involved. To become more effective in this area, we suggest the following:

Become aware of the effect of drop-in visitors. For one week, keep a list of every drop-in visitor you have and the approximate time spent with each. Total the time, put a dollar figure on an hour of your time, and then compute the cost of your time spent. Follow the same process for estimating the value of the visitors' time. Now compute total estimated cost of the drop-in meetings. Then ask yourself if you are being "cost effective."

Decide whether or not the demand of the drop-in visitor warrants interruption of your work. Sometimes you may really want to talk with the visitor—at other times you may not. In cases of the former, make the person comfortable, but not so comfortable that he or she wants to stay. Stand up and remain standing. Do not offer a seat. If asked if you are busy, reply, "Yes, but we can take a couple of minutes to talk." During the conversation, edge the visitor toward the door.

Some key sentences to use to reduce the time wasted by drop-in visitors might be, "I am scheduled for something in five minutes (or give the actual time)." Or, "Gee, thanks for stopping by. Please make an appointment for some time next week when we will have more time to spend talking." You might respond to a drop-in parent by saying, "We really need to talk about this longer than time will allow now. Let me have my secretary set up an appointment for us. (You are standing and edging toward the door.) Thank you for understanding my tight schedule."

Drop-in visitors could be salespersons, parents, students, bosses, colleagues, police, and a multitude of others. Regardless of who they are, let us remind you: Remain In Control! You should be comfortable enough and secure enough to implement the suggestions in this section no matter who the visitor is.

Salespeople are notorious "drop in's." Some districts do not permit salespeople in the schools without prior clearance through the central office. This prevents them from being unexpected interruptions. In most systems, however, there is no central purchasing so the principal does have to see salespeople in order to make intelligent decisions pertaining to new materials. Do you know how many educational sales representatives and fund-raising representatives there are in your area? The Educational Sales Representatives' Association of Maryland, the District of Columbia, and Delaware had 156 representatives listed in their 1979–1980 directory.[1] Add to this a probable 150 or so representatives who are not listed and you could be dealing with over 300 drop-in visitors in this one category.

Once you let them in the door, you probably will not be free in less than an hour. Do you have 300 or more hours to spend with sales representatives? Let them know that you will not be available on a drop-in basis. If you need to see sales representatives, tell them you will make contact with them for an appointment.

Most educational publishers and major suppliers exhibit at the key conventions. In order to keep up-to-date on new textbooks and materials, try to attend one of the leading conventions yearly.

Your secretary can employ most of the methods mentioned for dealing with drop-in visitors. This includes being aware of the teacher who has a couple of minutes to kill and plans to kill them with the principal. That may be a good use of the teacher's time, but it probably impinges on the principal's. Remember, you are in control, so if you succumb to any drop-in visitors, you do so only because you want to.

GET THE MONKEYS OFF YOUR BACK

How many times do administrators try to be all things to all people? When this is done, additional responsibilities are added to an already overwhelming workload. Be supportive, of course, but do not try to solve everyone's problems.

An effective principal is one who is aware when he is accepting responsibility for the actions of others. Unfortunately, many of us feel a personal responsibility for *everything* that goes on in the school. Whether it is a fight or an inappropriate action on the part of a teacher—somehow we feel personally accountable. This can become a very serious problem for time management. We must learn to do the best we can to ensure that the school runs as smoothly as possible without personally taking every routine task on ourselves. Remember, everyone is responsible for his or her own behavior. Do not let others hold you responsible for things over which you have little control or influence.

Remember the following:

- Help others to do their jobs, but be sure *they* take responsibility for handling their problems.
- Students, teachers, parents—all those with whom you work—need to know that they have responsibilities, too.
- Define the boundaries of your authority, and the responsibilities that others have.
- Do not accept blame for problems caused by others.
- Clarify roles among parties involved in conflicts—what can each do to help solve the problem?

---

[1] Educational Sales Representatives Association of Maryland, District of Columbia, and Delaware, Inc. *Directory of Educational Sales Representatives* (1979–1980).

DELEGATING RESPONSIBILITY MAY BE YOUR BEST TIME SAVER[2]

The entire concept of decentralization is formed around delegation of responsibility *and* authority. This becomes more evident as one moves upward in the hierarchy. There should be a direct relationship between the amount of delegation and the level of the administrator, as shown in Figure 4-1.

Figure 4-1

PERCENT OF DELEGATION

(Association of California School Administrators, 1979)

90 — Superintendent
75 — Assistant Superintendent
50 — Principal
25 — Assistant Principal

For most principals, failure to delegate becomes the most significant cause of poor time management. The administrator must always remember there are assistants, teachers, and secretaries who can help him or her save time. The administrator cannot possibly perform adequately all tasks for which he or she is ultimately responsible.

In a poll of several hundred executives from a cross-section of business and industrial firms, the following reasons were given for not delegating more often:[3]

My subordinates lack the experience.

It takes more of my time to explain than to do it myself.

A mistake by a subordinate can be costly.

My position enables *me* to get faster action.

There are some things I should not delegate to *anyone*.

My people are already too busy.

My subordinates just are not ready to accept more responsibility.

I am concerned about lack of control over the subordinate's performance when I delegate to him.

I like being busy and making my own decisions.

The use of a chart as illustrated in Figure 4-2, p. 90, should be helpful in determining to whom activities could be delegated.

---

[2]Parts of this section have been adapted from "An Update on Time Management," *Operations Notebook No. 8,* February 1979 (Association of California School Administrators).

[3]L. Steinmetz. *The Art and Skill of Delegation.* Reading, Massachusetts: Addison-Wesley, 1976.

Figure 4-2

DELEGATION LOG

(Keep in your notebook)

Date	Activity	Should It Be Delegated?	If So, To Whom?

Be sure to delegate, but remember that the final responsibility falls back on you. Therefore, know your people well before delegating responsibility. When you decide who is capable of handling a particular responsibility, give that person as much as he or she will take.

Contingency planning was discussed earlier. It is known that certain emergencies will arise, but it is not known when. For example, a student comes into the office with a badly cut leg. Is there a contingency plan for this emergency? Does everyone know what has to be done and by whom? Such a plan could include delegation of particular responsibilities; the secretary might notify the proper people, and another staff member might be responsible for first aid procedure in such an emergency. As a result of planning and delegating, everything goes like clockwork. If the administrator is not aware of, and does not implement, such planning devices, great harm as well as time loss may result. The time-conscious administrator should periodically review all contingency plans with the people to whom responsibility has been delegated to be sure they are still necessary and workable.

One of the most frequent "excuses" given for not delegating is, "If I want a job done right, I had better do it myself." This is one of the biggest causes of work overload. This myth is used by the administrator who cannot turn loose and must have a hand in everything. This administrator also works late, takes work home, and has a staff morale problem because staff members are not given enough (or any) responsibility. There is no way everything an administrator is expected to do can be done well if the administrator attempts to do it alone. Instead, the administrator will do those things that he or she does well, but neglect many other important tasks because there is *not enough time.*

The school administrator should do those tasks for which he or she has particular strengths and competencies. It is a rare administrator, indeed, who can claim expertise in every aspect of the job. Delegating parts of the tasks to others saves time and uses support staff effectively.

In the interest of managing time wisely, it may be best for the principal to do the tasks that he or she enjoys and thus completes more quickly. Frankly, it is no sin to delegate what you do not like to do or are not interested in doing.

Other tasks that could be delegated are those not in a state of flux. As change agent, the administrator should continue dealing with tasks concerned with change. Delegate and forget standard operating procedures.

If administrators really believe they do not delegate because they cannot trust their subordinates to do the job right, they have no one to blame but themselves. They usually employ their assistants or other subordinates, and should make their selections with the job responsibilities in mind. Employ the person who can handle those responsibilities you want delegated! If you are taking over for another administrator and the assistants are already on board, sit down with them to delineate their responsibilities as well as your expectations. You may have to provide periodic guidance, but in the long run, it will save you time. Allow them to make mistakes and in fact tell them that you expect it. Otherwise, they may not do anything for fear of making one. This will foster a feeling of trust and improve overall performance. It should be remembered that subordinates often avoid responsibility because they lack self-confidence.

Keeping in mind that decisions should be made at the lowest level possible, ask what subordinates can and should do. To have optimum efficiency, administrators must learn what and how to delegate. If an entire task cannot be delegated, perhaps part of it can be.

Not having enough time to train people in various functions frequently seems to be a problem for principals who do not delegate. On the contrary, we believe that administrators who are concerned about time management do not have the time *not* to train subordinates. Hours spent now in working with subordinates will give you days in the future. In order to spend 80 percent of your time on the 20 percent of the priorities at the top of your list, you must delegate.

The administrator could delegate tasks that need skills he or she has already mastered, thus broadening an employee's skills. Of course, this requires analyzing the job and the skills of the assistants. Delegating does involve some risks, but it is on-the-job training and may be very effective in-service. This leads to the growth in ability of your staff; and as you delegate more, your own ability to delegate also grows.

In summary, we recognize that it is easy to describe how to delegate, but hard to practice for both you and your subordinates. It will take time initially, but will pay dividends in time saved if you persist. It may be an important contribution to your professional growth as well as to the growth of your staff.

Establishment of a list of priorities does not mean they must all be done by you. Not only can many tasks be *done* by others; they may frequently be *done better* by others. In addition, there are some routine tasks that could be delegated—tasks not even identified as priorities— that are now being done by you.

Delegation of responsibility is essential for the maximum utilization of time. If the majority of time is devoted to the few key priorities, what happens to the not-so-important many? As they are on your list, they are important and must be addressed.

For all items, you should ask, "Who is best equipped to handle this?"—"Who can be trained to do so?"

HOW TO SAY NO TO TIME-CONSUMING EXTRAS

Quite often we take upon ourselves time-consuming chores that we should avoid. If a teacher has a certification problem and asks us about it, we are inclined to say, "I do not know, but I will check on it for you." There goes another slice of your time. Or, a teacher says to you, "Johnny has not turned in his homework all week. I do not have time to check on it. Would you please call his mother to find out why?" At this rate, you will not have any time for your own priorities. We have listed ten suggestions that will help school administrators say no to time-consuming activities that do not move them toward completion of their major priorities.

1. Realize what is being asked of you.
2. Think about the consequences of saying yes.
3. Determine why others are asking you rather than someone else or themselves.
4. Think about whether or not you are a "soft touch."
5. Ask, "Why me?" when you are asked to do something.
6. Project the amount of time you will need to respond to the request if you say yes.
7. Say no but give an alternate suggestion.
8. Reroute the request to someone else (delegation, remember?).

9. Never promise what you cannot deliver.

10. Simply say no.

DEALING WITH YOUR BOSS

In order to make the most efficient and effective use of time, school administrators must know their boss well. The principal must establish a good working relationship with his or her boss. Time to spend with the boss must be structured just like all the rest of your time. Make it clear at the beginning of your association that your primary function is to serve the children, so you may not always be immediately available when called by the boss. Do not stop everything and clear your calendar every time the boss drops in unannounced or comes forth with a whimsical idea that has no relationship to your priorities.

If this is the way the boss actually operates, he or she must feel your priorities are less important. You should try to establish a positive comfort level by determining with the boss his or her expectations for principals and the procedures for communicating. This will help you feel more secure, and enable you to admit failure and ask for help.

To resolve time-wasting problems caused by miscommunications or such things as those listed above, we need to take a hard look at relationships with our boss. First, we need to learn to put ourselves in his or her shoes. We should try to ask ourselves, "If I were the boss, what would my expectations be for principals?" Try to answer that question objectively, and develop a set of expectations from the results.

Second, it is up to you to initiate discussions and other communications relevant to your school with the boss. This can be done by brief, periodic notes asking for clarification of expectations, by scheduling brief meetings together, or by setting up visits to the school at a time that is mutually convenient. The point here is that *you* should take the initiative.

Finally, you will eventually need to establish, on a regular basis, ways to review specific expectations, procedures, and activities. A good time to do this might be during or before your evaluation if you have one. The best way, however, is to *start* the job assignment by asking for a meeting to clarify expectations. You will want to ask what is wanted of you but also be sure to ask for some things *not* wanted. Make lists of both. This will help establish and clarify boundaries.

The following steps will help establish clear understandings with the boss:

1. Develop a list of specific management tasks you think you will want and need to do.

2. Ask the boss to review the list indicating those items with which he or she agrees and those with which he or she does not.

3. Ask the boss to list other management tasks.

4. Discuss the list together, set goals, and come to agreement.

STRESS FROM OVERLOAD OR HOW TO BE KILLED BY TIME

When the factors discussed in this chapter become excessive and out of control, you begin to feel the negative aspects of stress. This is an important reason for getting control of your time. Stress is neither always good nor always bad. It is a stimulus that has an effect on bodily functions. Dr. W. B. Cannon was the first to study effects of stress on the body.[4] The body has the same reaction when a person is in front of a large group making a speech and when a person is confronted by a mugger. This reaction has become known as the "fight or flight response." The body tenses in seconds to either stand and fight or to run away. This is the same response that causes a cat to hunch its back and raise its hackles.

The brain senses a stressor. Pupils dilate, blood pressure increases, and production of stress hormones increases. It is the increase of blood pressure and increased production and distribution of hormones that could cause problems. A person who is in a constant state of stress arousal is more likely to develop hypertension, headaches, ulcers, heart disease, diabetes, and colitis.

Dr. Hans Selye describes the fight or flight response as the alarm reaction. This is the body's attempt to maintain normalcy.[5] If the stressor ceases to be a factor, the body returns to normal. However, if the stressor continues, it will create a great deal of wear and tear on the body. Excessive, continued exposure will eventually lead to exhaustion. It is during this stage that the diseases mentioned will begin to manifest themselves.

Several ways to deal with the negative effects of stress include practicing good time management, avoiding situations that have a continued negative impact, changing the situation, and learning relaxation techniques.

The subject of stress management is far too complex to be handled adequately, nor is this the purpose of this book. We strongly suggest attendance at one of several stress-management workshops that are available. A positive approach to stress management, and a more thorough knowledge of it can make your life more enjoyable as well as help you manage your time much more effectively.

CONCLUSION

The techniques discussed in this chapter have enabled us to be free from overload. The same results can be yours. Pro-active planning will lift the overload burden from your shoulders, so that it will no longer be necessary for you to sit at your desk waiting for something to happen so you can react.

---

[4]W. B. Cannon. *The Wisdom of the Body*. New York: W. W. Norton, 1932.
[5]H. Selye. *Stress Without Distress*. New York: J. B. Lippincott, 1974. *The Stress of Life*. New York: McGraw-Hill, 1956.

Chapter 5

Establishing Time-Saving Procedures in Working with School Discipline

To choose time is to save time. —Francis Bacon

INTRODUCTION

A time-consuming area for school administrators is that of pupil discipline. This is not an area that is amenable to shortcuts, no matter how tempting that may be.

Many books have been written about discipline, including philosophical discussions, classroom management techniques, reward and punishment systems, legalities, rights and responsibilities, and the development of elaborate psychological and sociological theories.

Since we are doers and implementers, we will concentrate on discipline in this section from the perspective of effective and efficient time management.

DISCIPLINE THROUGH THE WRITTEN WORD, OR IGNORANCE OF THE (SCHOOL) LAW IS NO EXCUSE

We find time used most efficiently and effectively when dealing with disciplinary problems if we have a school-wide *Discipline Policy* prepared jointly by staff, parents, and students. Such a policy should include a philosophy, an infraction list, a list of consequences, and a student appeal procedure. We have designed our own for our schools with positive goals, attitudes, and expectations toward pupil discipline. Naturally, rights and responsibilities must be included.

From the time-management perspective, time spent in developing a school-wide discipline policy accomplishes much. Such a policy provides a basis for disciplinary actions to be taken by teachers and principals, it helps assure consistency in handling discipline, and it gives us a basis to monitor, review, and evaluate the effectiveness of the school's disciplinary procedures.

An excellent example of a statement of rights and responsibilities is shown in Figure 5-1, p. 96.

The checklist in Figure 5-2, p. 97, is provided to assist you in establishing or improving your school's approach to discipline. Check each item that applies.

PROCEDURES

A primary consideration when developing a school discipline policy is to develop procedures that are clear, consistent, and workable. The keys with respect to time management are whether or not the procedures help accomplish the goals and whether or not the procedures are efficient.

In a recent study of time spent by high school assistant principals on discipline, the names of students and referring teachers were logged from September through January. This brief study shows several interesting findings.

Students referred in September for discipline continued to be referred during the five-month period. It became clear that actions taken by the assistant principals with their pupils in September did not significantly deter those pupils from wrongdoing later on. Of course, there could be many reasons for this, but one major reason could be that the actions taken were short-term, immediate punishments that appeared to have little long-term effect on behavior change. As a result, much valuable time was spent on "repeaters." It is important, while developing procedures, to seek long-term solutions.

Figure 5-1

RIGHTS AND RESPONSIBILITIES OF MEMBERS OF THE MARK TWAIN COMMUNITY

Members of the Mark Twain Community have the:

- right to be mentally and physically safe;

- right to expect that their personal or community property will not be abused, destroyed, or stolen;

- right to be in a learning environment free of disruption;

- responsibility to observe the laws regarding the possession, use, or transfer of drugs at Mark Twain Community;

- responsibility to follow the policies on smoking as established by the Board of Education;

- responsibility to follow their programs and to participate as appropriate; and

- right to expect that their property, including money, will not be taken from them through threats (extortion) or games of chance (gambling).

Figure 5-2

CHECKLIST FOR DEVELOPING AN EFFECTIVE SCHOOL DISCIPLINE APPROACH

Behavior Expectations and Values

- 1. Expectations protect significant human rights.
- 2. Values are translated into clear standards (desirable behavior) and limits (undesirable behavior).

Communicated Expectations

- 3. Staff, students, parents have involvement in establishing expectations.
- 4. Staff, students, parents know (make commitment to) operational expectations.
- 5. School-wide standards and limits are consistently supported by all staff and volunteers.

Strategies for Prevention of Discipline Problems

- 6. Staff use several effective techniques for promoting desirable behavior.
- 7. Staff use several effective techniques for reducing undesirable behavior.
- 8. School schedule provides regular small-group discussion time with advisors or counselors.

Strategies for Developing Student Coping and Conflict-Resolution Skills

- 9. Staff encourages "adult" transactions and avoids sending "you-blaming" messages to students.
- 10. School curriculum includes instruction in coping and conflict-resolution methods.
- 11. School provides appropriate due process procedures for disciplinary actions.

Strategies for Reaction to Behavior Disruptions

- 12. School implements a continuum of disciplinary reactions, from least to most extreme.
- 13. Continuum is established and implemented with student, parent, and staff involvement.
- 14. Continuum includes option for immediate, nonpunitive crisis or disruptive behavior intervention.

Consultation, Support, and Staff Development Activities

- 15. School has ongoing consultation and support available for staff, students, parents, and SARD (School Admission Review and Dismissal team).
- 16. School arranges priority staff in-service programs for effective discipline.

Feedback and Evaluation

- 17. School identifies and assesses progress on overall, school-wide behavior goals.
- 18. School provides for continuous progress reporting to students and parents on student social and behavior goals.

The findings also indicated that most of the referrals were from a few teachers. More training in behavior management for these teachers would help to reduce the assistant principals' workloads, thus giving them more time to devote to other school priorities.

Figure 5-3, p. 99, lists several techniques that could be discussed during a faculty meeting or PTA meeting devoted to behavior management.

Figure 5-3 contains some suggestions only. No matter what procedures are agreed upon, be sure to discuss them in detail with all the people who could be affected—staff, students, and parents.

IS THIS THE PAPERWORK THAT FINALLY BREAKS YOUR BACK?

Remember the section in Chapter 3 entitled "How to Stop Paperwork from Breaking Your Back"? A third important guideline for time management as it relates to discipline is to implement efficient methods of handling paperwork.

We are including some representative forms in this section for you to peruse and adapt for your own situation. While examining these samples, we suggest you use the following questions to help you analyze their worth:

1. Do the forms provide an efficient method to help develop positive movement toward established discipline goals, yet resolve the immediate concern?
2. Do the forms enable the school to document pupil, teacher, and administrative actions?
3. Do the forms conform to due process and legal requirements?
4. Do the forms provide copies to pupils, parents, and teachers?
5. Do the forms show consistency with district rules and expectations?
6. Do the forms indicate follow-up processes when needed?
7. Do the forms indicate resources that can be provided to pupils, parents, and/or staff?

Figure 5-4, p. 101, could be used for attendance concerns. The teacher completes the top section and the appropriate office staff completes the bottom section. Multiple copies provide immediate feedback as well as documentation. Figure 5-5, p. 102, also deals with attendance but is completed only by teachers and is more specific.

Figures 5-6, 5-7, and 5-8 provide a quick but simple method for teachers to refer a student to appropriate office personnel. Perhaps more important, they require the pupil to be more deeply involved in resolving the problem. See pp. 103, 104, and 105.

Any time there is a serious disciplinary infraction, the student should have the right to give his or her impression of what took place. Figures 5-7 and 5-8 are ways that could be used to obtain, in writing, the student's reaction to the disciplinary report made by the teacher.

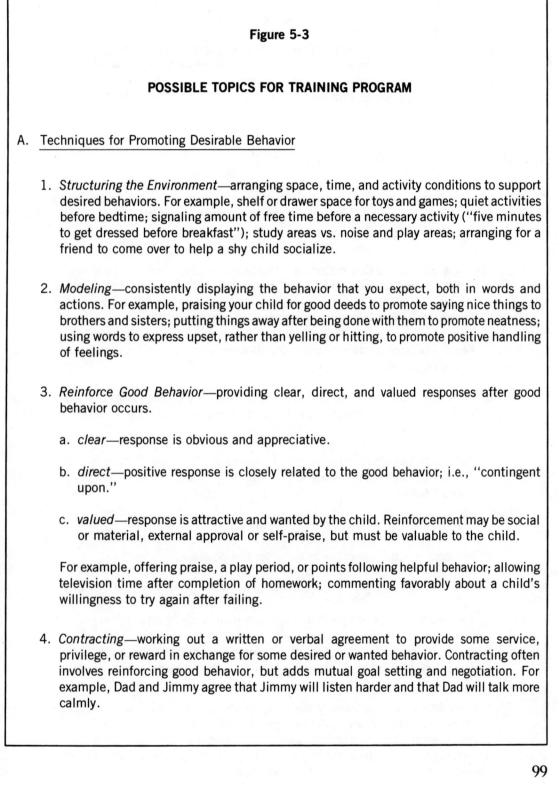

Figure 5-3

POSSIBLE TOPICS FOR TRAINING PROGRAM

A. Techniques for Promoting Desirable Behavior

1. *Structuring the Environment*—arranging space, time, and activity conditions to support desired behaviors. For example, shelf or drawer space for toys and games; quiet activities before bedtime; signaling amount of free time before a necessary activity ("five minutes to get dressed before breakfast"); study areas vs. noise and play areas; arranging for a friend to come over to help a shy child socialize.

2. *Modeling*—consistently displaying the behavior that you expect, both in words and actions. For example, praising your child for good deeds to promote saying nice things to brothers and sisters; putting things away after being done with them to promote neatness; using words to express upset, rather than yelling or hitting, to promote positive handling of feelings.

3. *Reinforce Good Behavior*—providing clear, direct, and valued responses after good behavior occurs.

    a. *clear*—response is obvious and appreciative.

    b. *direct*—positive response is closely related to the good behavior; i.e., "contingent upon."

    c. *valued*—response is attractive and wanted by the child. Reinforcement may be social or material, external approval or self-praise, but must be valuable to the child.

    For example, offering praise, a play period, or points following helpful behavior; allowing television time after completion of homework; commenting favorably about a child's willingness to try again after failing.

4. *Contracting*—working out a written or verbal agreement to provide some service, privilege, or reward in exchange for some desired or wanted behavior. Contracting often involves reinforcing good behavior, but adds mutual goal setting and negotiation. For example, Dad and Jimmy agree that Jimmy will listen harder and that Dad will talk more calmly.

Figure 5-3 (cont'd)

5. *Regulated Permission*—arranging or providing socially acceptable ways to express troublesome feelings and impulses. For example, allow child to smack a Bozo doll when feeling like hitting somebody; give child paper and crayons to draw how he or she feels when really angry; send child outside to shout when child needs to make noise.

B. Techniques for Reducing Undesirable Behavior

1. *Setting Limits*—providing a clear-cut statement of rules or expectations. For example, hitting is not allowed in this house; you are not permitted to break things; you must sit still while I am driving.

2. *Stating and Enforcing Consequences*—indicating what will happen if the rule or limit is not followed, and following through with the stated penalty if a violation occurs.

   – Consider the following principles for stating consequences:

   a. *Feasibility* (how practical)—example, "If you cry once more . . . I'll strangle you" vs. "I'll send you to your room."

   b. *Relevance* (how related to violation)—example, "If you take things that don't belong to you . . . I'll have to keep you out of football practice" vs. "I won't let you use them when you ask."

   c. *Reasonableness* (how fair or extreme)—example, "If you aren't home on time . . . you won't be allowed out of the house for a month" vs. "You won't be allowed to go to your friend's house tomorrow."

   – Consider the following principles for enforcing consequences:

   a. *Immediacy*—the sooner the better after the violation.

   b. *Nonpunitiveness*—giving the penalty not to hurt or get revenge but to teach a lesson.

   c. *Consistency*—making sure that the penalty is enforced for all violators and violations.

   d. *Fostering responsibility and choice*—helping child see that choice was his; reminding child that decision to violate is up to her but has unpleasant consequences.

3. *Planned Ignoring*—intentionally tolerating an unwanted behavior because it is: (a) relatively minor and temporary, (b) to be expected in the situation, (c) typical of a particular developmental stage. In addition, planned ignoring can be effectively used along with reinforcing the more desirable behavior. For example, not paying attention to an argument between siblings, and quickly praising them for getting along a little bit later.

Figure 5-4

ATTENDANCE DISCREPANCIES

(To be completed and sent to the office any time a discrepancy is noted)

☐ Present but listed absent   ☐ Absent from class

Pupil _____

Subject _____

Period _____   Section _____

_____   _____
            Teacher   Date of Discrepancy

- -

Action Taken By Office

_____

_____

                    ☐ Excused
Record Absence as:
                    ☐ Unexcused

                                     _____
                                              Administrator

For Office
Send:
Copy 1—To attendance officer
Copy 2—To teacher
Copy 3—To counselor

Figure 5-5

UNEXCUSED CLASS ABSENCE REPORT

Student's Name _____ Homeroom Section_____

Subject _____ Teacher _____

Date(s) of Unexcused Absence(s) _____ Period _____
                                 _____ Period _____
                                 _____ Period _____

Action Taken by Teacher:
_____ 1. Conference with student   _____ 3. Parents contacted
_____ 2. Detention assigned   _____ 4. Referred to Assistant Principal
        Dates:_____   _____ 5. Referred to PPW (Pupil Personnel Worker)
               _____   _____ 6. Other: _____
               _____   _____
                                                 _____

Student Initial _____

Comments: _____

_____

DISTRIBUTION: WHITE/Teacher
                GREEN/Assistant Principal   _____
                YELLOW/Parent   Teacher's Signature
                PINK/Counselor
                GOLD/Student Folder

Figure 5-6

PUPIL REFERRAL

NAME (Last, First) _____ Section _____ Teacher _____

Time Sent _____ Period _____ Date _____ Subject _____

Grades Last Six Weeks
  (Where Applicable) _____ This Six Weeks _____

Please Check

☐ Failure to conform to class procedures   ☐ Lunch conduct   ☐ Smoking

☐ Disrespectful   ☐ Hall conduct   ☐ Other (Explain)

☐ Willful disobedience   ☐ Fighting

To Be Completed in Office—Action Taken

☐ Conference with student   ☐ Parent conference   ☐ Excluded from class

☐ Detention   ☐ Referred to counselor   ☐ Suspended

☐ Called parent   ☐ Referred to Pupil
                                 Services   ☐ Other (Explain)

Figure 5-7

PUPIL'S EXPLANATION OF REFERRAL

Name (Last, First) _____   Age _____ Section _____ Date _____

Address _____   Phone:
(Parent's Business) _____

_____   Phone:
(Home) _____

Sent by _____   Subject _____   Period _____   Time _____

My grade in this subject last six weeks: _____   Counselor's Name: _____

1. Explain in your own words the reason why you were sent to the office.

   _____

   _____

   _____

2. What do you think is a possible solution to this problem? _____

   _____

   _____

To be completed by office:

Action taken: _____

   _____

Figures 5-9, p. 106, and 5-10, p. 111, are both examples of forms used in connection with specific consequences. Detention is a common form of discipline in secondary schools. A student contract is an excellent way to get the student involved in changing his or her behavior.

Figure 5-8

THOMAS S. WOOTTON HIGH SCHOOL

STUDENT ADJUSTMENT—STATEMENT OF SITUATION

Name of Student _____ _____ _____
                          (Last)   (First)   (Age) (Date of Birth)

Homeroom Teacher _____ Homeroom Section_____ Date _____

Sent to Office by _____ Period _____ Time _____

Your Counselor's Name_____

Fill in your regular schedule:

Period:	1st	2nd	3rd	3rd or 4th	4th	5th	6th
Subject							
Teacher							
Room No.							

Parent's Name_____ Home Telephone _____

Address _____ Work Telephone_____

_____
                    (Zip)

Statement: Give details of the situation, both from your viewpoint and the viewpoint of your teacher.

_____

_____

_____

_____

_____

_____

Figure 5-9

THOMAS S. WOOTTON HIGH SCHOOL

MEMORANDUM: DETENTION

First Period Teacher* _____

Please give to this student.

TO: _____

Remember you have detention _____ 2:40–3:30 p.m., Room 146 (Typing Room). You must be on time with study materials or you will not be admitted and time will be doubled. Failure to attend without permission from me is a *suspendable offense.* You must see me before 2:30 p.m. the date if you cannot attend.

Student Signature _____

*Teacher—please return to Miss Jones's mailbox when student has read and signed.

Thank you,

Miss S. Jones
Assistant Principal

106

Of course, no discipline policy will be effective unless parents are deeply involved. Figures 5-11, p. 112, and 5-12, p. 113, are two excellent examples of letters to parents informing them of disciplinary concerns.

MONITOR THE MONITORS

Finally, be sure to take time to monitor the system of discipline being utilized. When evaluating your school's discipline policy, think about whether it is helping the school to reach its goals. Keep perspective. Think about the long-range impact of what is being done. Some discipline problems are beyond our expertise. When this happens, ask for help. At the same time, help others to obtain necessary skills.

Mrs. Floretta McKenzie, Superintendent of Schools in Washington, D.C., has written the following thoughts about discipline:

Remember that the *goal* of discipline and education is self-discipline; thus, discipline is a matter for instruction rather than enforcement.

Discipline is the ability to identify the essential character of a situation or circumstance, to determine one's most constructive role in it, to carry out that role directly and to sustain it as long as necessary. Such skills are learned, not enforced, and should be a part of the curriculum. Discipline is best taught by persons who are willing to impose it upon themselves.

When understood and implemented fully, the classroom can operate on two rules: (1) No one can disrupt another's learning, and (2) Everyone has responsibility for asking questions until he or she clearly understands.

The goal of a teacher must not be a quiet classroom but a learning environment.

1. Develop and talk over with students definite guidelines of what is acceptable classroom behavior. Help them know how they can "change things around here" through constructive channels.

2. Know each child well enough to know how he or she will usually react to a situation, to know what procedure will or will not work. "Cut the cloth to fit the pattern."

3. Make your discipline as private as possible.

4. Be careful about boxing yourself into a corner. Private disciplining can often help to prevent this.

5. Show a child that you do not condone vulgar language, but do not interrupt a lesson for a lengthy harangue about it. If you rob vulgar language of its shock value, it is often discontinued.

6. Praise good behavior. Children want acceptance. Try to show that good behavior is the way to be accepted.

7. Humor often relieves tension.

8. Report good as well as bad work to parents.

9. Get to know parents, and help them to know you.

10. When children are working in groups, make some provision for a slow child to get some help from another child when he or she falls behind. This will prevent interrupting the teacher, but will also not force the child to sit and wait for long periods of time to get help. This strategy can prevent many problems.

11. Avoid sarcasm and ridicule. They usually result in hostility rather than improved behavior.

12. Try to foresee a confrontation and prevent it from developing. Once expectations are clearly stated (privately, if possible), the teacher's most constructive action is to "get out of the scene."

13. Avoid hostile physical contact. Try to convey a message by means of eye contact, a hand gesture, a glance, or a whispered word.

14. Be careful not to let a minor issue become a major crisis. Don't give an issue more attention than it deserves by overreacting or escalating.

15. When you begin to get angry, hold on and cool off before acting. Know yourself and your touchy spots.

16. Remember that a child needs to save face. Try not to put the child in a situation where he or she will lose face in front of peers. When the child is in a tight spot, try to give him or her an opportunity to save face. Teach the child more about himself or herself.

17. Apologies, to be meaningful, should be spontaneous—duress should never be employed. Apologize for your actions whenever necessary, helping the child to see how humans err.

18. There should be consistency to your expectations of student classroom behavior. The approach, however, to the enforcement of rules of classroom behavior will vary with the individual.

19. In actual practice, your position is always tenable. The child never perceives of himself or herself as able to win with an adult. Understanding and accepting this premise, you need never feel the necessity of competing with a child and winning.

20. Practice what you preach—courtesy, respect, observance of safety rules, etc.

21. When a confrontation develops, analyze the situation to see if you handled it well. Ask your peers or your principal to react to the situation and tell how they might have handled it.

22. If you make a mistake, admit it to the class. Students respond positively when they realize that the teacher is human.

23. Avoid disrupting the whole class for an individual incident whenever possible. It is costly to stop instruction for an entire class.

24. Extra assignments as a means of disciplining a child should be avoided.

25. Teaching each child at his or her appropriate instructional level reduces frustration and often avoids confrontations.

26. Try to help a child to understand and accept his or her limitations. A child should never be humiliated.

27. Try to handle deviant behavior through education rather than punishment whenever possible.

28. Criticize the act rather than the child. This is an unusual activity and a very difficult one for most people. Ask someone to sit in and observe or tape record your session with the child so that you can get constructive feedback.

29. Provide *success* experiences for each child regardless of the grade label on the door.

30. Let the class help take some responsibility for plans. Pupil-teacher planning helps to set a good classroom climate.

31. Be able to laugh at yourself.

32. Establish classroom procedures so that children will know what to expect.

33. Be firmer the first few weeks than you hope to be later; in other words, demonstrate that you will enforce rules with no equivocation. This eliminates "testing behavior" and helps the child to know his or her environment.

34. Strive for a high degree of participation by all pupils. Ask yourself: (1) Who does most of the talking in your class? If you do, you're talking too much. (2) Am I providing opportunities for involving all children in every lesson?

35. Try not to create situations that encourage children to challenge your authority.

36. Listen to a child's side of any troublesome situation. It is important to hear what the child has to say. Develop a strategy, however, to allow the class to proceed. Then, once the class is occupied, proceed with the child. (Once a child knows you intend to talk with him or her, the child is better able to wait.)

37. Try not to create situations that provide a child with no choice but to lie. Skilled and understanding questioning will most often lead to the truth.

38. Don't threaten anything you can't carry out—better yet, don't threaten.

39. To be most effective, discipline must be carried out as soon as possible. If a parent conference seems advisable, arrange one as soon as possible, preferably going immediately to the home.

40. Be on hand when the bell rings with prepared lessons and materials well in advance of their use.

41. Secure pupils' attention before starting a lesson. Begin your class promptly. No plan is perfect. Have alternate plans and materials to fill unexpected gaps.

42. Avoid interruptions: when your students have started working on a project, avoid interrupting them. Unnecessary interruptions create distractions that can lead to trouble.

43. Give assignments of homework that provide a significant learning experience and of such character that the pupil can do the work without a lot of assistance. Don't give homework if you don't make provisions for either classroom or teacher evaluation. A child should always know you have evaluated all assignments. Build in guarantees of success as often as possible.

44. Corridor control cannot be one teacher's job . . . it's every teacher's job *all the time.* While one teacher cannot do it alone, it takes only one teacher to destroy it. Whether you are on duty or off duty and whether the students are yours or someone else's, help take responsibility for general school-wide discipline.

45. Student behavior can be stimulated by physical surroundings. Therefore, have the room environment working for you, not against you, in establishing good classroom discipline.

46. Keep marks and discipline separate and apart.

47. Don't forget the substitute teacher. Teach your students early in the year what their attitude, behavior, and responsibilities should be when you are absent.

Figure 5-10

THOMAS S. WOOTTON HIGH SCHOOL

STUDENT CONTRACT

_____, _____ grade, will be permitted to attend
Wootton School as long as the student will:
1. Attend all classes with no unexcused absences and/or tardies.
2. Have a letter from his or her parents whenever it is necessary to be out of school or late to
   school for medical or dental appointments, etc.
3. Be responsible for the school's procedures as outlined in the Student Handbook.
4. Attend all detentions as assigned, 2:40–3:30 on day assigned.
5. Not leave school grounds without office and parent permission.
The terms of this contract will be in effect until June 16. If the above conditions are violated,
_____ will be suspended for _____ days and referred to Mr. Pat,
Department of Pupil Services (for counseling in order for him or her to be) / (with a recommendation that he or she not be) readmitted to Wooton School.
I have read the above Student Contract and agree to meet the terms as stated.

_____   _____

cc: Parent/Guardian
    Counselor, Wootton School
    Mr. Pat, Pupil Services Office
    Student's File

Figure 5-11

SCHOOL ATTENDANCE AND/OR DISCIPLINE NOTICE TO PARENTS

Date _____

REASON:

☐ Discipline   ☐ Unexcused absence   ☐ Tardy to class

☐ Excessive absences   ☐ Tardy to school   ☐ Other

TO THE PARENT OR GUARDIAN OF _____
                                      Name of Student

The progress of your child in school depends greatly on regular attendance and proper classroom behavior. We ask your cooperation and support on this matter. Please respond by returning the reply portion of this letter or call me at 555-4444 as soon as possible.

Please be advised that:_____

_____

_____

                                        Teacher_____

                                        Class_____

DETACH AND RETURN

REPLY BY PARENT:_____

_____

_____

Signature _____ Date _____

DISTRIBUTION: WHITE/Parent; YELLOW/Attendance Secretary; PINK/Counselor;
               GOLD/Teacher

112

Figure 5-12

THOMAS S. WOOTTON HIGH SCHOOL
NOTICE OF POSSIBLE FAILURE

Dear Parents:

Student_____ Grade _____ Date _____

A check of your child's marks indicates that he/she is doing near failing work in the following

subject: _____.

The most apparent reason(s) are:

____ Assignments not well prepared   ____ Guidance and correction resented

____ Class time wasted   ____ Work not commensurate with ability

____ Poor class participation   ____ Failure to report for needed help

____ Poor test results   ____ Too many absences

____ Disturbing influence on class   ____ A course change should be considered

A ninth grade student must pass English and two other academic subjects as a minimum requirement to be promoted to grade 10. To be promoted to the 11th grade, a pupil should have a minimum of seven academic units of credit. To be promoted to the 12th grade, a pupil should have a minimum of eleven academic units of credit. For students pursuing the college preparatory course, grades of "C" or better are necessary. If any student receives a mark below "C" as a final grade, summer school will be recommended. If a student receives "E's" for two or more reporting periods in the second semester of a full-year course, he shall receive an "E" for the year.

Good school performance stems from cooperative effort shared by the school and the home. This letter is sent as a reminder that unless greater effort is made on the part of the student, only a failing or very low mark can be expected.

You are invited to make an appointment to come to the school to discuss your child's work or work habits with me and/or the counselor.

Some Study Suggestions for Student:

1. Carry an assignment notebook and list all work to be done.
2. Take books and other appropriate study materials home.
3. Study at least 20 minutes per subject—if no specific assignment, then review.
4. Ask for help at school—make an after-school appointment to see the teacher.
5. Organize your day—there is a time for work, for play, and for study.

_____
Teacher

CONCLUSION

It has been our intention to provide a few suggestions to increase your effectiveness in time management as it relates to discipline. Many concepts discussed in other parts of this book are also applicable to this subject and should be transferred and incorporated wherever you think appropriate.

Chapter 6

Time-Saving Techniques in Selecting, Supervising, and Evaluating Staff

*Time flies, all right, but during working hours it often seems
to be head winds—Luke Neely*

INTRODUCTION

We believe strongly that selecting, supervising, and evaluating staff is the heart of the job of the school administrator. This means principals must find techniques to ensure the best use of time, not simply the use of the least amount of time. Shortcuts in this process only for the sake of saving time should not be the major consideration.

Unfortunately, most theorists and authors in the area of staff supervision do not recognize the severe time demands placed on principals that prevent them from adhering to detailed, time-consuming supervisory tasks. What is needed is a clear understanding of what is important, and of specific, simple strategies for principals to use during various phases of supervision.

In this chapter, we will present several simple, but powerful, techniques to help principals get the most out of time spent on this important area of their responsibility. We will show how gathering of performance data can best be accomplished through the use of long-range planning and task orientation.

Evaluation of teacher performance should be looked upon as a positive process. It should be structured with the goal of improving instruction. Only as a last resort should it be used as a disciplinary measure or for dismissal. Documentation, hearings, and appeals required for dismissal are counterproductive and consume a great amount of time. This same time could be better utilized to improve overall instruction if an outstanding job is being done in selecting, supervising, and evaluating staff.

USING STRUCTURED INTERVIEWS TO HELP SELECT STAFF

The beginning point in staff supervision and evaluation is in the hiring process. It is extremely important to time management to select staff members as carefully as possible. This chapter will help improve your selection skills to assure employment of teachers strong in subject matter, teaching skills, and interpersonal relationships.

In some school districts, principals do not make hiring decisions. We believe that no one knows the community, students, and needs of the school as well as its principal. Therefore, the local school administrator should make hiring decisions, but he should also be able to demonstrate the ability to make effective choices.

One way we can help ensure selection of competent staff is to use a structured interview. In this process, we ask all applicants the same questions and rate them on their responses. Those with the highest rating we recommend for employment.

Plan ahead. To save time, we follow these steps:

- Prepare for the interview to the same degree the applicants are expected to prepare.
- Think about the desired characteristics.
- Commit those characteristics to writing.
- Develop thought-provoking questions from a list of characteristics.
- Refrain from including questions that can be answered with a simple yes or no.
- Share the questions with staff members who will be affected by your selection.
- Ask for, and accept, their suggestions.
- Consult with a colleague who is well qualified in the specific field under discussion.

Whenever possible, we conduct the interview with a team comprised of ourselves and representative staff members who have a particular interest in the position. Each member of the interview team has a copy of the same rating sheet to judge each candidate on every question asked. After each interview and before going on to the next, the score sheet is tallied, without discussion among team members.

At least three people should be interviewed with an understanding that the principal has the final choice between the top two interviewees according to the ratings.

Figures 6-1, 6-2, 6-3, and 6-4, pp. 117–124, illustrate several interview forms that we have developed and used successfully, following the guidelines just discussed. They include an example for a regular education teacher, a learning disabilities teacher, a special education aide, and a secretary.

Figure 6-1

INTERVIEW FORM (ELEMENTARY CLASSROOM TEACHER)

NAME: _____ PHONE: (work) _____ (home)_____

What degrees have you earned? (5 points)

What institutions granted the degrees? (5 points)

Award each response a point value no higher than six. Total all points at the end of the interview.

1. Tell us about your employment experiences.

2. How would you familiarize yourself with the curriculum?

3. How would you group your students for instruction?

4. How would you determine the students' instructional levels?

5. What method of teaching reading do you prefer?

Figure 6-1 (cont'd)

6. What is your chief objective as a teacher?

7. What role do you see for specialists (music, art, p.e., reading, speech, etc.)?

8. What techniques would you use for behavior management?

9. How would you design the physical setting of your classroom?

10. What training have you had in teaching exceptional children?

11. What background do you have in math, social studies, and science?

12. In what ways would you establish and maintain communications with parents?

TOTAL POINTS: _____

COMMENTS:

Figure 6-2

INTERVIEW FORM (LEARNING DISABILITIES TEACHER)

NAME: _____ PHONE: (work) _____ (home)_____

What degrees have you earned? (3 points)

What institutions granted these degrees? (3 points)

Award each response a point value no higher than five. Total all points at the end of the interview.

1. Tell us about your employment experiences.

2. What do you see as your strengths?

3. Describe what each of these means to you and how you would relate these skills to your instructional program. (5 points each)
   a. Language
   b. Visual/motor
   c. Prereading
   d. Auditory skills
   e. Reading
   f. Math

4. What techniques would you use for behavior management?

5. How would you design the physical setting of your classroom?

Figure 6-2 (cont'd)

6. What balance do you envision between your role in direct intervention with students and your role as a resource to teachers?

7. What diagnostic instruments (name and purpose) would you use most frequently?

8. In what ways would you establish and maintain communication with classroom teachers?

9. How do you deal with your own frustrations in teaching children with learning problems?

10. In what ways would you establish and maintain communications with parents?

11. How would you utilize a paid aide? A parent volunteer?

TOTAL POINTS: _____

COMMENTS:

Figure 6-3

INTERVIEW FORM (LEARNING DISABILITIES TEACHER AIDE)

NAME: _____ PHONE: (work) _____ (home)_____

Award each response a point value no higher than seven. Total all points at the end of the interview.

1. Please tell us about any formal or informal training you have received to work with learning disabled children.

2. Tell us about your employment experiences.

3. How do you perceive your role as an aide to a learning disabilities teacher?

4. What strengths would you bring to this position?

5. How would you establish and maintain communications with the teacher?

Figure 6-3 (cont'd)

6. What ways would you use to cope with frustrations of working with learning disabled children?

7. What is your familiarity with these mechanical aides? (7 points each)
   a. Typewriter
   b. Ditto machine
   c. Mimeograph
   d. Copying machines (Xerox, etc.)
   e. Audio-visual equipment

8. How would you deal with directions or a situation that you did not understand?

9. What is your perception of a learning disabled child?

10. If a learning disabled child's parents approached you for information, how would you respond?

TOTAL POINTS: _____

COMMENTS:

Figure 6-4

INTERVIEW FORM (SCHOOL SECRETARY)

NAME: _____ PHONE: (work) _____ (home)_____

Award each response a point value no higher than seven. Total all points at the end of the interview.

1. Tell us about your employment experiences.

2. Please tell us about any formal secretarial training you've had.

3. What is your familiarity with the following office skills and equipment? (7 points each)
   a. Typing
   b. Shorthand
   c. Copying machines (Xerox, etc.)
   d. Ditto machine
   e. Stencil/mimeograph machine
   f. Filing
   g. Dictaphone
   h. Telephone

Figure 6-4 (cont'd)

4. What would you do if a parent called and asked for information about a teacher or child?

5. What group would you consider to be the most important group in the school?

6. What experience have you had in maintaining records such as accounts, checking, and payroll?

7. If you have worked in a school before, what were your specific tasks?

TOTAL POINTS: _____

COMMENTS:

STAGES OF EFFECTIVE PERSONNEL SUPERVISION AND EVALUATION

After the hiring process, an effective personnel supervision and evaluation system must be established. It should include the following stages:

- Getting organized for supervision
- Observation of employee in action
- Analysis of data gathered
- Conducting feedback conference
- Wrapping it up, closure, and next steps

Within each of these stages, the principal must find efficient methods to carry out supervision. Let us examine each of these more carefully.

Stage I: Getting Organized

First, you should obtain a list of competencies for teacher performance either from the district office or by generating one with your staff. From this list of competencies should be determined specific things to look for in terms of employee performance. During this process, examples of unacceptable performance should also be identified.

For example, one of the stated competencies may be, "the teacher provides for student involvement." In this case, the principal could look for ways in which the teacher (a) plans

---

Figure 6-5

EXPECTANCY: PROVIDES FOR STUDENT INVOLVEMENT

Teacher, please answer yes or no to each of the following questions which we will then discuss.

Do you:

1. Plan lessons based on what students are expected to do (as opposed to what content will be covered or what material will be presented)?

    yes _____ no _____

2. Provide students (often) with a choice of learning activities?

    yes _____ no _____

3. Routinely involve students in planning or selecting activities?

    yes _____ no _____

4. Routinely ask students for their opinions about the effectiveness of learning activities?

    yes _____ no _____

lessons based on what students are able to do, (b) gives students choices of different learning activities, (c) routinely asks students for their ideas and input, or (d) asks students what they think about the instruction.

A sample form that you could use to help generate discussion with a teacher about these specifics is shown in Figure 6-5, below. This form includes items to which teachers are encouraged to give a candid response and can then be used in discussion with the principal to establish common expectations. (Please note that Figure 6-5 is an abbreviated form that includes only one competency from among many possible competencies.)

In using a form such as 6-5, the principal could meet with a group of teachers from a department or grade level, have them complete the form, and have an open discussion about the results. Differences should be ironed out resulting in agreement on a clearly stated list of expected teacher behaviors. This agreement is essential to good supervision, and promotes understanding and good communication *before* the supervisory process begins.

It is imperative that people being supervised know the "game plan." They must know the criteria upon which the evaluation will be based, how often a formal observation will be made, what input will be used in addition to the instructional criteria, and the level of the evaluator's expectations. Expectations should be set high, but they also should be attainable. Research studies have shown repeatedly that people tend to produce at the level of expectancy set for them by their leaders. Remember, you and we are their leaders. Be sure the staff is aware of your expectations and demand that they be met. The school administrator sets the tone.

It is a good idea to schedule a periodic staff meeting (at least yearly) to have the evaluation procedures explained. Share the evaluation form that will be used and the type of notes that will be taken during an observation. Let teachers know that all records pertaining to evaluation are open for individual inspection. Reiterate as often as necessary that the entire procedure is geared toward improving instruction. After all, why do schools exist?

After establishing expectations and procedures, a written schedule of classroom observations and conferences will need to be developed. Since we have discussed at some length the importance of long-range planning, we are reiterating here the necessity of establishing this schedule as early in the school year as possible (even before school begins, if possible). Plan for all observations by blocking out times on the calendar throughout the year. This does not mean that you cannot observe at other times. To the contrary, times should be built in to carry out additional observations in case they are necessary. Work backward using deadlines established by the school district, allowing ample time and leeway. Once the observation times have been established, inform your secretary and your supervisor. They will help remind you to follow through on those observation commitments you have established.

Figure 6-6, p. 127, provides an example of an observation and conference schedule. Simply list the names, the number of required observations, and, if someone else will be observing other than yourself, the name(s) of those other observers. Then list the dates of the week of the anticipated observation and conference. Be sure to transfer those dates to your calendar. Space the observations throughout the year so you do not set for yourself unreasonable or unattainable workloads in any one month.

In summary,

- Review and define the competencies for effective performance.
- Identify the specific behaviors you expect and those you do not want.

Figure 6-6

SCHEDULE OF OBSERVATIONS AND CONFERENCES

Teacher	No. Obs. Req'd.	Observer	1		2		3		4		5	
			Obs.	Conf.	Obs.	Conf.	Obs.	Conf	Obs.	Conf.	Obs.	Conf.

- List sources of information, examples of observable behaviors, and other anticipated evidence for effective performance. Decide on a method to gather and record the data.

- Communicate expectations with persons you are supervising so they understand all of the above, as well as the procedures being used to supervise them.

- Develop a written annual schedule for supervision.

Stage II: Observation of Employee in Action

Most of you have learned, through experience and training, ways of gathering data about employee performance. This may have included exposure to various methods of gathering classroom information such as Flander's Interaction Devices, Goldhammer's Clinical Supervision, and others. From our perspective, many of the current data-gathering methods fail in three significant ways. First, most models are too complicated to use in classroom observations. Second, many instruments force us to gather impressions or "judgments" rather than help determine specific teacher behaviors. And, finally, most methods are much too time-consuming for us to use.

Observers should be able to do at least two things as a result of a classroom observation. First, they should be able to reconstruct the lesson, including the sequence of instructional activities used by the teacher. Second, data should be in specific behavioral terms, giving concrete examples of what the teacher did, and what the pupils did. Any method used to gather classroom data should also be simple and easily used as a basis for discussion and for making objective judgments about the teacher's performance

The principal should be looking for support that the teacher is meeting the criteria that have been established and that they are being accomplished to the level expected. The data collected must relate to the criteria, and should be the basis for judgments made. The absence of data in a given area does not necessarily imply negative performance.

Another excellent method for gathering data is to make a videotape or audiotape of the lesson and analyze the playback with the teacher. This allows both the observer and the teacher to pick out nuances that could not otherwise be noted.

Accuracy in gathering data is extremely important. When gathering classroom data, the observer must be on task every moment. He should be attentive to each pupil behavior and to each activity of the teacher.

Remember,

- Record data, not judgments.
- List observable behavioral examples.
- Cite evidence of performance.
- Keep a record of performance data and information.

Stage III: Analysis of Data

A primary task for principals is to make judgments about teacher or support staff performance. As indicated earlier in this chapter, we urge you to always try to form such judgments on the basis of specific data, gathered in an open, understood manner. During the entire process, the employee should be kept fully informed.

After every classroom observation, a feedback conference should be planned and conducted to discuss the data that have been obtained. In planning for a feedback conference, follow these guidelines:

- Outline a purpose for the conference.
- Prepare to explain and/or defend the purpose.
- Develop a way to display and discuss data from the observation.
- Decide on a way to obtain agreement on authenticity.
- Plan a strategy to obtain concurrence on conclusions drawn from analyzing the data as to strengths and weaknesses of the lesson.
- Sketch a preliminary plan for improving one or more aspects of instruction, including resources required, time, and the focus of the next observation.
- Be prepared to help the teacher understand and agree to each element of the plan.
- Plan a method to conclude the conference.

Stage IV: Conducting the Feedback Conference

When conducting a feedback conference, principals should always:

- Review expectations and roles.
- Share and discuss data gathered.
- Identify specific resources for help.
- Agree on next steps—what to do as a result of the conference feedback.
- Restate, modify, or clarify expectations and roles.

In Stage IV, the supervisor has to implement the strategies decided on in Stage III. In doing so, we have had success utilizing Paul Hersey and Kenneth Blanchard's appealing leadership concept called "Situational Leadership Theory."[1]

Hersey-Blanchard Leadership Model

We have shared with you a number of situations throughout this book that require utilization of specific leadership skills. To a great extent, the style used in a given situation is determined by the characteristics of the person(s) involved. The same style could be used, for example, with two different people and be effective with one but have no success with the other.

The Hersey-Blanchard Situational Leadership Theory is based on the amount of direction and socioemotional support which must be provided by the leader and the level of

---

[1]P. Hersey and K. H. Blanchard. *Management of Organizational Behavior: Utilizing Human Resources*, 4th ed. Englewood Cliffs, NJ: Prentice-Hall, Inc., 1982.

maturity of the follower. The amount of direction is called task behavior, and the socioemotional support is referred to as relationship behavior.

In task behavior, the leader is involved in one-way communication by informing the follower what must be done as well as when, where, and how the task is to be performed. In relationship behavior, the leader is involved in two-way communication, giving socioemotional support and psychological strokes.

Four leadership styles have evolved: High Task-Low Relationship; High Task-High Relationship; Low Task-High Relationship; and Low Task-Low Relationship. The leadership style employed is determined by the maturity level of the individual or group. If the maturity level is low, the leadership style is High Task-Low Relationship (telling). As the maturity level increases, leader behavior moves to High Task-High Relationship (selling), Low Task-High Relationship (participating), or Low Task-Low Relationship (delegating) for a very mature individual or group.

Followers with low maturity tend to lack both the willingness and the ability to perform the task, so one should use the High Task-Low Relationship style.

Followers who are motivated but do not have the ability are considered to have low to moderate maturity, so a style of High Task and High Relationships is used.

Moderate to high maturity is exhibited when the follower has the ability to complete the task but is not willing. The appropriate style for this group is participating or Low Task-High Relationship.

High follower maturity calls for a style of Low Task-Low Relationship, or delegating. This is for the group or individual who is willing and able to perform specific tasks.

Delegation of responsibility was discussed at great length in Chapter 4. Quite often it is heard that administrators tried delegating but the person to whom a task was delegated failed to follow through. The problem may be that the wrong leadership style was used. A style of Low Relationship-High Task may have been used, assuming a high level of maturity when another style may have been more appropriate. Remember, the leadership style must fit the situation.

Using these concepts, the supervisor should vary the amount of task and relationship behavior used in providing feedback to a staff member. Generally speaking, the supervisor should use a High Task-Low Relationship style in working with an immature follower. As the follower becomes more and more capable of doing the job, the supervisor should provide less task behavior and more relationship behavior. Ultimately, though, the supervisor should move to a Low-Low style, enabling the follower to assume full responsibility for doing the job.

Stage V: Wrapping It Up, Closure, and Next Steps

Following the conference, you should review what has or has not been achieved. The following questions may help in this process:

1. Did the conference include all the elements wanted?
2. Was the format appropriate for the situation?
3. Was the desired climate achieved?
4. Was there anything that should have been added that had not been thought of before the conference?

5. Was there anything that should have been omitted?

6. Were the objectives accomplished?

7. Was anything unintended accomplished?

8. What tasks are left undone?

9. How could the conference be conducted differently if it could be done over again?

Prepare a written summary of the conference, and provide a copy for the other participant. Do not be all talk and no action. Follow through on training resources and any other help you promised. Monitor progress of the employee regarding agreements reached during the conference.

This is also the time to review your own behavior and practices used in *all* phases of the supervision process. What could you do to become a more effective supervisor? How could your system be improved?

KEEPING THE RECORD STRAIGHT

In order to ensure due process for employees and in order to save time if your process is questioned, you should keep careful written records of everything that may pertain to an evaluation. This would include, of course, data from all observations and follow-up conferences as well as other conference notes and letters about the employee. Be sure the employee has seen all such materials and have them initialed to indicate that they have been seen.

Figure 6-6, p. 127, the schedule for observations, could also be used to help with the record keeping. On the second line adjacent to the teacher's name could be listed the actual dates (in a different-colored ink) the scheduled observations and conferences were completed.

CONCLUSION

There are probably as many supervision styles as there are principals supervising. The administrator should acquire as much theoretical background as possible, and then pick and choose to develop his or her unique style.

It must be kept in mind that the purpose of supervision is to increase teacher effectiveness. The teachers were selected by you because of the way they performed during the structured interview and your impressions of their knowledge of the subject area. You probably also felt that they could motivate and stimulate the students as well as transfer knowledge to them. Does the performance support your judgment? Is the teacher meeting your expectations? The information collected, the way it is collected, the way it is shared with the teacher, and the relationship established all contribute to the leader's supervisory style.

You must decide if your style is effective. This can be determined by answering the following questions:

1. Is each teacher formally observed by an administrator at least twice every school year?

2. Do your actions support the statement that the purpose of the evaluation process is to improve instruction?

3. Do you have a clear record of all observations?

4. Has a conference been held within a reasonable amount of time (three school days) following an observation?

5. Are strengths in teacher performance pointed out as well as areas that need improvement?

6. Are teachers' performances improving yearly as they gain experience?

7. Is every teacher on the staff average or above?

8. Do you confront the teacher who does not exhibit the expected level of competency?

9. Are all administrators in your school expected to adhere to the same standards?

10. Is dismissal action initiated for the employee who simply does not meet competency levels regardless of help given?

Time spent wisely here will save an inordinate amount of time later that would be spent either defending a weak teacher to parents or losing a hearing because correct procedures were not followed.

Chapter 7

Maximizing Output by Minimizing Time Spent in Meetings and Conferences

Time is what we want most, but what, alas!
we use worst—William Penn

INTRODUCTION

Time spent in meetings and conferences can be either one of the greatest time wasters encountered by administrators or one of the greatest assists given to an administrator. Which it is depends on several factors and suggestions that will be discussed in this chapter.

We will discuss when to have a meeting, why to have a meeting, alternatives to having meetings, techniques for conducting meetings, and how to analyze productivity of meetings.

WHEN TO HAVE A MEETING

Recently, while talking with an executive of a packaging firm, we were told that all top managers and department heads met for a half day each week. The purpose of these meetings is to monitor production. Imagine the planning and development that might be accomplished if these people did not spend so much time at meetings.

Quite often, a meeting is viewed as a sort of status symbol. "Last week I went to five meetings." "I have been asked to serve on another committee, so that means I will have at least one more meeting every week." "The superintendent wants me to go to that conference next month about remedial reading." Time spent at all these meetings may make us seem very important, but the loss of all this irretrievable time may also contribute to stagnation and ineffective job performance. Remember, one key principle of effective time management is to establish priorities.

We, as working administrators, have often attended meetings that are being held just for the sake of having a meeting. It was suggested earlier in this book that all prescheduled meetings be put on your calendar at the beginning of the school year. These could include meetings with the superintendent, faculty meetings, team meetings, subject coordinator meetings, and on and on. When you come to one of these meetings on your calendar, ask yourself the purpose of the meeting. If you cannot discover a purpose that is central to your highest priorities, do not attend the meeting. This will also keep you from appearing on someone else's time waster's list. Of course, we are not advocating insubordination to your superiors, so if you are really *required* to attend, by all means, do so.

Meetings should be held when the business cannot be efficiently handled in any other manner. Meetings can be an efficient method of obtaining input for a decision based on open discussion.

Meetings should be held when there is a need to clear the air. As principals, we have all made decisions that have generated much negative reaction. This is a time to gather everyone together to talk about it. It will be time well spent. Give your rationale for making the decision and encourage discussion about it. The staff must know what is affecting you, and you must know how your decision is influencing them.

Similarly, meetings should be held to encourage a free exchange of ideas, concerns, or problems among staff members. We have all attended meetings where the most valuable time was the break. This is because it provides time for us to talk with colleagues and share ideas or discuss mutual concerns. This suggests a value in setting "agenda-free" meetings occasionally. There may have to be some ice-breaking activities to establish the mood, but after those, the leader should just stand back and "let it happen."

Meetings should serve two basic purposes. First, information needs to be conveyed from one source to others or shared to obtain common knowledge about something; second, managers use meetings as a method to involve others in decision making.

Remember, meetings should be called when there is a definite purpose, and when that is the most efficient way of accomplishing a task. Maybe a satisfactory decision can be made without pulling a lot of people together. Schedule it only if the issue cannot be resolved in any other way. If a meeting is not needed, then everyone's time is wasted and productivity is lost.

HOW TO ARRANGE AND CONDUCT MEETINGS AND STILL MAKE THE BEST USE OF TIME

If it does become necessary to call a meeting of staff, pupils, parents, or others, make sure the meeting is conducted efficiently. Nobody likes to feel that time is wasted in boring, endless discussions over trivial matters. We have listed below the major points to which you should conform when planning or conducting a meeting. Each will be discussed in more detail.

1. Purpose
2. Agenda
3. People
4. Location
5. Materials
6. Timing
7. Discussion

Time spent in meetings for which you have responsibility can, and should, be controlled. You determine the meeting content, who should attend, how it will be conducted, and when it will occur.

Have a Purpose

We cannot emphasize too strongly that meetings should always be held for a specific reason. The purpose should be stated in writing and distributed to prospective participants well in advance, whenever possible.

Always Set an Agenda

The agenda should be published and distributed with the stated purpose. During the meeting have it posted on newsprint or projected with overhead projector.

Use the agenda to keep track of progress. List business that was not completed at previous meetings at the beginning of the agenda. Use one column of the agenda to keep notes such as necessary follow-up, new policies, dates to complete an action, and names of people responsible for completing tasks. When the meeting is over, have this copy of the agenda duplicated and distributed the next school day. (See Figure 7-1 for an example of an agenda.)

Figure 7-1

SAMPLE AGENDA

Faculty meeting for March 2, 1982
    3:15 p.m - 4:15 p.m.
Participants—all teachers who teach reading and/or handwriting.
Purpose—In-service for revised curriculum in reading/language arts.
Please bring reading and handwriting curriculum guides.
Leader—Ms. Deborah, Reading Teacher

Time	Topic	Notes
3:15 p.m. (20 minutes)	Handwriting Guide	
3:35 p.m. (10 minutes)	New Units	
3:45 p.m. (5 minutes)	Tests for Novel	
3:50 p.m. (15 minutes)	Indicators of Implementation	
4:05	Review and Summary	

Invite Only Those People Needed

Only those people who might be affected by decisions reached as a result of a meeting should be involved. Be cautious of having the wrong people present or too many people or too few people. Consider delegating functions of the meeting to others if you are in charge. You may want to consider sending a subordinate if it is a meeting that may concern you but one that you may not have to personally attend.

If there is a program change that affects the social studies department, there is no reason to meet with the entire faculty. In this case, call a meeting of members of that department for a discussion of the change, and how it will affect that group.

During this meeting it may be determined that there are implications for the total school program. That is the time to call a meeting of the entire staff to examine, clarify, and finalize information.

Select an Appropriate Meeting Location

Select a location in keeping with the stated purpose; one that is free from interruptions, and one that involves the least amount of travel for the greatest number of participants.

Have "stand-up" meetings whenever appropriate. These are particularly useful for impromptu meetings that most likely will not have significant outcomes. "Stand-up" meetings will tend to discourage participants from long-windedness.

It is also a good timesaver to meet someplace other than your own office, such as the library or a classroom. This way you are able to leave at the conclusion of business. If the meeting is held in your office, you are stuck if any of the other participants want to stay around for a chat. Meetings in different classrooms also give the teachers a chance to share ideas by just being in other teachers' rooms.

Have Necessary Materials Readily Available

Tell people who will be attending the meeting what materials they should bring. These could be listed on the agenda. Also be sure to have all necessary equipment, such as audio-visual aids, on hand at the site of the meeting.

Set Times to Save Time

Put starting and ending times on the agenda as well as specific time limits for each of the discussion items. (See Figure 7-1, p. 135.) Stick to those times. Start on time. This will be positive reinforcement for those who are on time, and contribute to modifying the behavior of persistent late-comers. Do not go back over the agenda for those who are late.

Time limits on the discussion items will help control overzealous talkers. Assign someone to watch the time. Post a minutes-remaining chart and have someone keep it current. This reminds you and participants to stay on task.

As the leader, push the group toward closure, especially on difficult decisions. Groups are often hesitant to take definitive actions and may need prodding. If time honestly will not permit reaching a decision, consider appointing a subcommittee to return with recommendations at a future meeting.

To help a very verbal group stick to the established agenda time, give each member a certain number of tokens. Every time one speaks he must give up one token. When all his tokens are gone, he must stay quiet. This will help save time as well as put a little fun into the meeting.

Be sure to end the meeting on time. You can help yourself with this by scheduling the meetings right before something else for which participants have already planned.

Schedule the meeting when people whose participation you need can be there.

Structure the "Meat" of the Meeting

If it is your meeting, maintain tight control in order to stay on task. This is not a time for socializing. Expect adherence to the published agenda so that you are constantly moving toward accomplishing the stated purpose. Early in your tenure as a leader of this group, set your policy for meetings and let all staff members know. Try to allow no interruptions including messages.

Begin the meeting by reviewing decisions from previous meetings, if they pertain to the present agenda. Clarify items on the new agenda. Ask if any of the participants would like to add agenda items. Do so for those items the group sees as important.

Deal with highest priority items first. Consider having items of low priority handled by subcommittee. Some issues will be strictly informational and will require only presentation and clarification. Others will need in-depth discussion and decision making.

There may be issues that you will want to reserve for administrative decision. Explain to the group that you value their input and recommendations, but, as principal, you will make the final decision.

Summarize and review all decisions including staff assignments and deadlines. If you choose not to keep notes on the agenda for future reference, have minutes kept and copies distributed. Request status reports until assignments are completed. It is your responsibility to assure effective follow-up on the agreed-upon decisions.

USING MEETINGS TO INVOLVE OTHERS IN DECISION MAKING

An important role of the educational manager is making decisions. Principals and other school officials are concerned that adequate involvement take place in studying problems and determining the right course of action to resolve them. This is particularly true in working with community-related issues and developing faculty cooperation in implementing school policies. In this section, six techniques are summarized that could be used to help groups come to agreement on desirable goals, action steps, or solutions to problems. For each technique, a very brief description of the process is provided, with some advantages or disadvantages. Each of these will require an investment of your time, but in the long run will *save* you time by (1) providing structure for meetings, and (2) contributing to effective long-range planning.

I. Committee/Group Decision Making

One of the most popular approaches to involvement and group decision making is the use of a committee. You usually have the freedom to select the members of the group, can provide the degree of structure desired for the discussion process, and can control the extent to which the group recommendations are actually implemented in the school. The group process used most frequently is called consensus.

Ideally, consensus is a decision process for making full use of available resources and for resolving conflicts creatively. Consensus is difficult to reach, so not every decision will meet everyone's complete approval. Complete unanimity is not the goal—it is rarely achieved, but each individual should be able to accept the group decision on the basis of logic and feasibility. When all group members feel this way, you have reached consensus. This means, in effect, that a single person can block the group if he thinks it necessary; at the same time, he should use this option in the best sense of reciprocity. Some guidelines for use in reaching consensus are as follows: (a) Avoid arguing for your own position. Present your position as lucidly and logically as possible, but listen to other members' reactions and consider them carefully before you press your point. (b) Do not assume that someone must win and someone must lose when discussion reaches a stalemate. Instead, look for the next most acceptable alternative for all parties. (c) Do not change your mind simply to avoid conflict and to reach agreement and harmony. When agreement seems to come too quickly and easily, be suspicious. Explore the reasons and be sure everyone accepts the solution for basically similar or complementary reasons. Yield only to positions that have objective and logically sound foundations. (d) Avoid conflict-reducing techniques such as majority vote, coin flips, and bargaining. When a dissenting member finally agrees, do not feel that he must be rewarded by having his own way on some later point. (e) Differences of opinion are natural and expected. Seek them out and try to involve everyone in the decision process. Disagreements can help the group decision, because with a wide range of information and opinions, there is a greater chance that the group will hit upon more adequate solutions.

Advantages:

1. This process is used frequently, and people are aware of procedures. This is a democratic approach.
2. Opportunities exist for all members to have their say.
3. The creativity and results are limited only by the group members themselves.

Disadvantages:

1. The process can be dominated by a few persons.
2. Creative thinking is sometimes limited, because of group norms.
3. Conflict is sometimes minimized as an undesirable feature of interaction.
4. Some people get frustrated by the group process.

II. Structured Group Process

Using groups of 8 to 10 members each, participants using this technique could be asked to generate a specific action recommendation for consideration by the organization. This process, which can be used with groups of up to 100, is as follows: (a) Small groups are formed to study a specific problem area—naming the problem, identifying the conditions or causes of the problem, and generating specific action steps recommended to be implemented to resolve the problem. In writing the action recommendations, groups are asked to list who should do what, when it is to be done, etc. A group recorder prepares the recommendation on newsprint and acts as a spokesperson for the small group. (b) Recommendations from all groups are posted for review by the total group who have an opportunity to ask for clarification of each recommendation. (c) Small groups meet again and have an opportunity to revise or clarify their recommendation. (d) Recommendations are posted again in large group areas for action by a smaller decision-making group, which acts on each recommendation. (d) The decision-making group consists of all small group spokespersons, specifically designated officials from the organization (e.g., department director, associate superintendent, superintendent, etc.). The top-ranked official leads the decision-making process, and each recommendation is dealt with in front of other participants.

Advantages:

1. All participants have an opportunity to identify concerns and work on a specific action plan that indicates what, where, when, how, why.

2. Responsible authorities act on each recommendation in public, in front of the persons who developed the recommendations.

3. Because of the openness of the process, trust is fostered within the organization.

Disadvantages:

1. The process is difficult to manage, and requires skillful leaders who can intervene when necessary.

2. The unit leader needs to accept and agree to the process.

3. It is difficult for small groups to generate specific steps for the action plan; they tend to be vague. Skillful small group leaders help.

III. Nominal Group Process

This process is a deliberate, structured group approach, intended to identify goals and problems, generate information concerning a topic, or develop action plans. The structured process includes the following activities: (a) silent generation of ideas in writing, using 3″ × 5″ cards, (b) round-robin listing of all ideas on flip-chart, (c) serial discussion of ideas, (d) silent listing and ranking of priorities (preliminary vote), (e) discussion of vote, and (f) silent rerank and rating of priorities. The process could be used by a large group (50–100), broken into small groups (8–10) for most of the work. The process requires at least 3 hours for adequate completion, and all participants would need to work without interruption on the task—except for a brief break. With a large group (100), it is helpful for the leader to have several assistants, although this is not mandatory. The leader should have had experience in using the process for best results.

Advantages:

1. *All* participants have an opportunity to contribute ideas, criticisms, and suggestions. This process reduces influence of "vocals" in small group discussions who have a tendency to dominate and control the decision process in unstructured meetings.

2. A reading of the extent of agreement within the group is obtained through silent voting and a posting of the vote results.

3. The results are in print, public, and posted for all participants to see. This prohibits the leader from falsely interpreting group results after the meeting is over.

Disadvantages:

1. The process is time-consuming and requires commitment and adherence to the structure. This is frustrating for some individuals, and can cause conflict during the process.
2. The leader must have a clear understanding of the total process, be well prepared for each step of the process, have a grasp of the advantages and rationale for the approach, and have the skill to deal effectively with frustration on the part of some participants.

IV. Scenario Writing

This technique could enable participants, working alone or in a small group, to project future conditions and imagine that they are describing these conditions. Participants depict their vision of the future with as much specificity as possible, answering prepared questions, such as:

It is now the year _____.

What is your age?

What are your position and responsibilities?

List some of your daily activities.

What do you like about your work?

What two to three goals would you have for the year _____?

In using this technique, a wide diversity of "futures" is generated by respondents. The process could be used by small groups who would then have to come to agreement regarding the scenario.

Advantages:

1. The creative process generates some plausible pictures of future conditions. In the creative process, participants begin to see additional implications for present practices.
2. The process forces people to remove their prejudices toward the present; "pedagoguese" is limited.

Disadvantages:

1. It is very difficult and frustrating for some participants, and viewed as a waste of time.
2. Because so many varied scenarios evolve from larger groups, it is hard to manage or consolidate them.

V. Delphi Method

This technique is a method that could secure and collate opinions to project prospective future events and the approximate time of their occurrence. Also, a modification of this process has been used to help districts set budget priorities, and to identify communication and decision-making problems. The approach gives selected people an opportunity to identify future events that could occur; receive a collated summary of events identified by other respondents and indicate agreement or disagreement with various factors regarding each event; and, through successive rounds, the respondents are asked to provide written reasons for differing with the group median responses. The process includes the following steps: (a) Participants are segregated from each other—the procedure is frequently conducted by mail. (b) Each participant is asked to write out a goal or event that will, or may, occur at some time in the future. (c) All responses are collected and tabulated. A report is prepared, and goals or events generated are listed on a questionnaire to be returned to all respondents who reconsidered previous answers and all other events. Usually, the respondent is asked to respond to "date of occurrence," "impact," and "desirability," but other categories could be used. The completed questionnaires are again returned to all respondents who may revise responses giving specific reasons for deviating from total group median. (e) Proceed with additional rounds as above. Usually three or four rounds are sufficient.

Advantages:

1. The size of the respondent group can be as large as desired, limited only by the coordinator's time and expertise to tabulate, prepare, and handle materials.

2. A diverse listing of future events is obtainable by securing opinions from a wide population of participants.

3. A timetable is secured for planning.

Disadvantages:

1. The process is very time-consuming and requires considerable organization and tabulation of results, preparation, and distribution of materials.

2. Little opportunity is available for face-to-face discussion and resolution of differences or issue clarification.

3. Little opportunity is available for securing expert opinion. This process requires movement toward group norms, and does not protect the minority viewpoint.

VI. Charette

The charette technique is a problem-solving process by which neighborhood residents and local officials hold marathon meetings to discuss problems and decide on solutions. It is based on the assumption that interest and involvement breed dedication and responsibility. When used as a community participation process, the technique encourages positive communication between hostile groups, often resulting in more awareness and understanding. As a community planning method, the charette facilitates creative problem analysis and generation of agreement on implementable plans and solutions for neighborhood problems. Both objectives can be achieved in a compressed time period.

A steering committee is responsible for coordinating the charette process. This committee is different from the traditional steering committee in that it does not make policy decisions regarding any aspects of the community plan. It does provide technical assistance to the various work committees. The total number of participants in such a process could be several hundred, who are subdivided into work committees on specific topic areas. Each work committee is to examine and study problems or issues and generate proposed solutions to them. The results of their work, called "charette products," are discussed publicly by the steering committee, and are then submitted to other public officials for action or consideration. The process requires that participants work through the process, spread over several weeks, until products are derived.

Advantages:

1. Maximum citizen participation is encouraged through the expanded opportunity to get new ideas from a larger segment of the community.
2. Public officials see the process as a vehicle to focus on critical community problems.
3. Practical solutions to community problems are produced in a short time period.
4. Positive citizen participation is gained and plans are proposed for the entire community.

Disadvantages:

1. If uncontrolled, participants will not focus on important issues and reach practical solutions.
2. There is a tendency to present unrealistic demands that are in conflict with basic goals and/or for which funds for implementation do not exist.
3. Some citizens and neighborhood groups are not able to handle the direct responsibility to educate themselves on community issues and to act.

In this section, six distinct techniques for effective group involvement were briefly described. We have been involved in all of them either as leaders or participants. We recommend you try them. You'll like them! Each of these approaches has been used in school districts to study and resolve problems, generate community understanding and input, determine and project budget items and priorities, identify concerns, and develop recommendations to improve decision-making and communications practices.

ROLES PEOPLE PLAY IN MEETINGS

In conducting meetings, the leader must be aware of the dynamics of group activity. Participants frequently play roles, and sometimes behave in predictable ways. We, as administrators, should be aware of such possibilities and learn ways to handle effectively these situations and the conflicts that could develop during meetings. These roles, initially described by Boles, and then by Wedgewood are described in Figures 7-2, 7-3, and 7-4, pp. 143–144.[1]

---

[1]H. C. Wedgewood. "Fewer Camels, More Horses." *Personnel*, July/August, 1967.

Figure 7-2

The aggressor	Criticizes and deflates status of others; disagrees with others aggressively.
The blocker	Stubbornly disagrees; rejects others' views; cites unrelated personal experiences; returns to topics already resolved.
The withdrawer	Won't participate; "wool gatherer"; converses privately; is self-appointed notetaker.
The recognition seeker	Boasts; talks excessively; is conscious of his status.
The topic jumper	Continually changes subject.
The dominator	Tries to take over, asserts authority, manipulates group.
The special-interest pleader	Uses group's time to plead his own case.
The playboy	Wastes group's time showing off; story teller; nonchalant; cynical.
The self-confessor	Talks irrelevantly about his own feelings and insights.
The devil's advocate	More devil than advocate.

Figure 7-3

The initiator	Suggests new or different ideas for discussion and approaches to problems.
The opinion giver	States pertinent beliefs about discussion and others' suggestions.
The elaborator	Builds on suggestions of others.
The clarifier	Gives relevant examples; offers rationales; probes for meaning and understanding; restates problems.
The tester	Raises questions to test whether group is ready to come to a decision.
The summarizer	Reviews discussion; pulls it together.

Figure 7-4

The tension reliever	Uses humor or calls for break at appropriate times to draw off negative feelings.
The compromiser	Is willing to yield when necessary for progress.
The harmonizer	Mediates differences; reconciles points of view.
The encourager	Praises and supports others; friendly; encouraging.
The gatekeeper	Keeps communications open; encourages participation.

144

ALTERNATIVES TO MEETINGS

In the event that the main reason you have scheduled a meeting is to impart information that is not open for discussion, cancel it. Chances are strong that the same information can be shared in writing, and you won't take people's time simply to talk *at* them. In fact, we recommend that each agenda item be examined with this question in mind: "Can this be handled just as effectively by putting it in writing?" If the answer is yes, prepare a memorandum, thus using less of your time as well as your staff's time, since they can read it much more quickly than they can discuss it at a meeting.

Some principals write and distribute a weekly bulletin that lists items of importance and interest that need to be imparted to their staff. An example of a typical weekly bulletin is given in Figure 7-5, p. 146.

Another efficient method of accomplishing the purpose of a meeting without actually calling one is a conference call. We recommend this particularly for small groups of people who have difficulty scheduling mutually acceptable meeting times, or who have great distances to travel in order to get together. The telephone company can help make arrangements for a conference call.

MAKING MEETINGS WORTHWHILE

As in everything we do, the conduct of meetings we are leading should be periodically evaluated. Figure 7-6, p. 147, adapted from Bradford, Stock, and Horwitz could be used for evaluating meetings.[2]

Most of the form should be completed by the participants, and analyzed by you as the leader. We would use it several times with the same group in order to look for patterns of behavior.

Section One (I) helps you decide the type of environment in which decisions are being made. Of course, you may want different atmospheres depending upon your goals for the meeting.

The first part of Section Two (II) can be filled out by all group members and used by you to lead an evaluation discussion. Roles people play in meetings (Figures 7-2, 7-3, and 7-4, pp. 143–144) could be worked into this discussion.

Section Three (III) measures participants' reactions to meetings. We need to remind ourselves frequently, as principals, that wasting others' time is also a waste of our time. Section Three will help us keep this time factor in perspective.

CONCLUSION

Meetings are not to be taken lightly or for granted. They can be extremely valuable or head everyone's time-waster list. We hope that the ideas given here will help you in conducting efficient and effective meetings when needed.

---

[2]L. P. Bradford, D. Stock, and M. Horwitz, "How to Diagnose Group Problems," *Adult Leadership*, December 1953, 2 (7).

Figure 7-5

Weekly Bulletin

STONE ELEMENTARY SCHOOL

October 29, 1982

Friday Sheet

1. Title IX Complaints: Title IX complaints from employees and students may be submitted through one of the following ways:

    1. Follow Regulations 501-1, "Students' Involvement in the Educational Process," and 270-9, "Community Involvement: Inquiries and Complaints."

    2. Contact the coordinator for Title IX, Office of Human Relations.

    3. Contact the Regional Office of Civil Rights, Department of Education.

2. When you receive your report cards, you will notice a couple of changes as follows: On the kindergarten checklist, the objectives in the mathematics section have been updated to reflect the key objectives used with kindergarteners for ISM. In grades 1–6, a "year average" column has been added.

3. On Friday at 2:30, Ann, Norma, and I would like to meet with 4th–6th grade teachers and aides who work with ISM for a feedback session. The session will be held in the math lab.

4. Other upcoming faculty meetings will be:

    November 14th—Follow-up from the Nov. 7th half day in-service

    November 21st—Information from ITBS and CAT test data

    November 28th—K–3 teacher feedback session for ISM

5. There will be a PTA executive board meeting at 7:45 Tuesday evening in the lounge. Any interested staff member is welcome to attend.

The aim of this book is to make you more conscious of time and how to use it. We have dealt mostly with your time. In this chapter we attempted to show you how your actions could have an effect on others' time. Our final goal would be that, through you, your total staff would become more time conscious.

Figure 7-6

EVALUATION OF MEETING

I. Group Climate

What was the general group atmosphere? Place an × at the appropriate place on each line.

Formal_____._____._____._____.____: Informal

Competitive _____._____._____._____.____: Cooperative

Hostile_____._____._____._____.____: Supportive

Inhibited _____._____._____._____.____: Permissive

Open_____._____._____._____.____: Closed

II. Participation

1. How did you feel about your participation during that session? Circle one numeral.

1	2	3	4	5	6
Very satisfied	Quite satisfied	Somewhat satisfied	Somewhat dissatisfied	Quite dissatisfied	Very dissatisfied

2. Check a place on each scale that shows how you think others participated:

All people talked _____.1_____.2_____.3_____.4_____.5_ Only a few talked

All members involved ____.1_____.2_____.3_____.4_____.5_ All members uninvolved

All resources used _____.1_____.2_____.3_____.4_____.5_ Group failed to use most resources

The following questions on patterns of communication are best suited for an observer:

1. Who talks? For how long? How often?

2. Whom do people look at when they talk?
   a. Single persons: possibly potential supporters
   b. The group as a whole (scanning)
   c. No one

3. Who talks after whom, or who interrupts whom?

4. What style of communication is used (assertions, questions, tone of voice, gestures, etc.)?

Figure 7-6 (cont'd)

III. Group Effectiveness

The following questionnaire measures participant's reactions to a meeting.

Mark an × after each item in the box that best shows your reaction to this meeting.

	AGREEMENT Strong Mild	DISAGREEMENT Mild Strong
1. The results of this meeting were worth the time.	( ) ( ) YES! yes	( ) ( ) no NO!
2. I was given adequate opportunity to state my beliefs about subjects discussed by the group.	( ) ( ) YES! yes	( ) ( ) no NO!
3. Our meeting was efficient.	( ) ( ) YES! yes	( ) ( ) no NO!
4. I am satisfied with the attention and consideration that others gave to my ideas and opinions.	( ) ( ) YES! yes	( ) ( ) no NO!
5. We wasted too much time in this meeting.	( ) ( ) YES! yes	( ) ( ) no NO!
6. The group effectively used my knowledge of the subjects discussed.	( ) ( ) YES! yes	( ) ( ) no NO!
7. The most important topics were never discussed.	( ) ( ) YES! yes	( ) ( ) no NO!
8. I had adequate opportunity to influence our conclusions and decisions.	( ) ( ) YES! yes	( ) ( ) no NO!

Chapter 8

How to Save Time When Working with All Facets of the Organization

The longer the fiddle, the brighter the blaze.
Time is not for burning—Anonymous

INTRODUCTION

There are many individuals and groups in the school system requiring our time. Often, we have little or no control over these situations or groups. In preceding chapters we discussed the impact on time of such factors as dealing with your boss and drop-in visitors. In this chapter we will go into more detail about how you can gain and maintain control of organizational time.

WORKING WITH YOUR BOSS RATHER THAN FOR YOUR BOSS

Many school systems' organizational schemes demonstrate a very confusing structure and chain of command. Principals find that they are spending time responding directly to members of the board of education, the superintendent, assistant superintendents, directors, supervisors, and many others who assume positions of authority. Figure 8-1, p. 151, a typical organizational chart from a large school system, shows examples of the number of "bosses" with whom principals may conceivably interact.

Your school system's organizational chart should be studied and understood. Where do you fit in the hierarchy? Ideally, you should have only one boss. All directives, correspondence, and similar materials should come from or through that boss. This should eliminate or at least reduce time-wasting conflict in orders or expectations.

Anyone in the hierarchy can abuse our time, if allowed to do so. How much this can be controlled may depend upon the type of power one wields. We see two kinds of power— position power and personal power. Position power is obtained by a person because of the job assignment or rank. Personal power can be obtained through a charismatic style of leadership, reputation resulting from performing effectively, seniority, or personal influence or "connections." We are more likely to have negative impact on our time when we allow others to take from us position power vested in us by the organization. In effect, since they do not have official sanction for position power, they have increased their personal power over us, and made concomitant demands on our time.

School systems have goals and priorities that are published and widely distributed. Keep a list of these goals and priorities on the bulletin board next to your desk. When people in the chain of command are causing you to divert time from these published priorities, gently remind them about the time needed to devote to one or more of the system's goals. Perhaps such a reminder, if handled with grace and tact, will allow you to stay on task. Of course, some of your superiors may simply respond, "Handle it!" If this is the case, comply rather than be insubordinate. In other words, *know your boss!*

This means you need to make every effort to find out about his or her leadership style(s), values, and philosophy. Do you know what your boss likes and dislikes and the type of program he or she expects: The process of decision making, the preferred writing style, and the way he or she wants meetings conducted should be understood. Does the boss want you to be a workaholic? Is he or she a stickler for detail? The more you know about his or her characteristics, needs, and expectations, the easier it will be to effectively administer a school without wasting a lot of time redoing and explaining.

This does not mean you have to do what the boss would do or that you have to abandon your principles. No effective leader wants to be surrounded by clones of himself or herself. You can, however, make decisions while consciously knowing how much risk is involved. Check with the boss on some things, and act independently on others. You will save time if you have a sense of areas of agreement or potential disagreement that might exist between you and your boss.

Frequent, but efficient, communication with superiors is important. Most upper-level managers appreciate being well informed. You do not want to be a pest or ask for advice about everything, but you should make sure that your superiors know what you are doing and how things are going. If problems are likely to crop up concerning a program for which you are responsible, then your boss should be advised, and perhaps can give you ideas for solving a problem or can help by referring you to others who have already faced similar situations. Either way, this should help you save time by not having to "reinvent the wheel." The boss should *not* be the last to know about potential problems. Whenever possible, let him or her know beforehand.

Spend necessary time with your boss so that you both get a clear picture of the other's goals to help you understand the boundaries of your respective roles. A successful management team has a common, clear understanding of organizational goals and expectations and what is being attempted to fulfill them. So, too, must you and your boss have a common understanding and acceptance of mutual roles.

It is not necessary for you and your boss to use the same styles. It may even be healthy for the organization to support many different styles of administration.

You do not have to have all discussions in your boss's office. Invite him or her to spend time at your school. Do not feel you even have to talk with your boss every day or every week. Exchanging plans, thoughts, and requests in writing as much as possible may help save valuable time for both of you.

Someone once said, "You never respect your boss more than when you take over his job." Just as we do not want unjustified criticism from our teachers about our actions, we should try not to be unduly critical of actions of our superiors. We know it is difficult not to become cynical and waste time talking behind the boss's back, but when tempted to do so, try to put

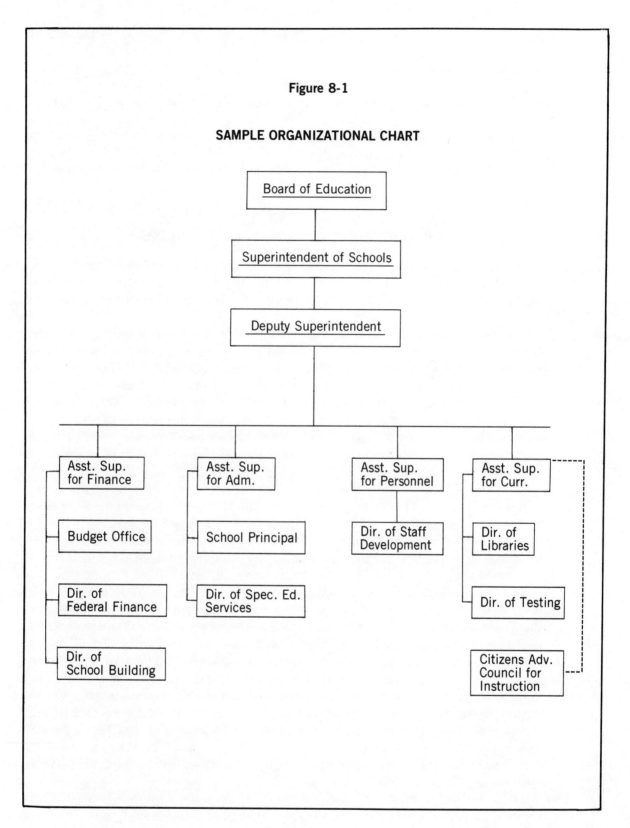

Figure 8-1

SAMPLE ORGANIZATIONAL CHART

Board of Education

Superintendent of Schools

Deputy Superintendent

Asst. Sup. for Finance

Budget Office

Dir. of Federal Finance

Dir. of School Building

Asst. Sup. for Adm.

School Principal

Dir. of Spec. Ed. Services

Asst. Sup. for Personnel

Dir. of Staff Development

Asst. Sup. for Curr.

Dir. of Libraries

Dir. of Testing

Citizens Adv. Council for Instruction

yourselves in the boss's shoes. Express differences openly and honestly when you have them and provide data, ideas, and suggestions. But after all is said and done, respect the decisions made by superiors. Remember, your superiors are doing their job, too, when they make decisions. That is their responsibility.

The best way of dealing with your superiors is to be the best school administrator in the district. If you do an outstanding job in all aspects of school administration, and this is evident, you will earn "personal power." When you do, those above you will leave you alone to do the outstanding job they know you can do.

TIME-SAVING SUGGESTIONS FOR WORKING
WITH TEACHERS AND OTHER IN-SCHOOL SUPPORT STAFF

Chapter 4 went into detail about working with teachers. Chapter 6 discussed interviewing, selecting, supervising, and evaluating staff. This section will deal with how staff relationships and the overall health of an organization can affect morale, effectiveness, and the use of your time.

If teachers are permitted to feel superior and, through their actions, make custodians, secretaries, and aides feel like second-class citizens, jealousies will most likely erupt between professional and support staff. If this is allowed to go unchecked, there will be counterproductive behavior that will eat away at the time you should be spending on high-priority items.

It is important that an atmosphere be established that is conducive to good teaching and learning. All members of the staff are there to provide the best possible education for the children. This requires a clean environment, materials that are available when needed, typing that is accurate, and teaching time that is not wasted on cleaning, preparing materials, or typing because of unhealthy staff relationships.

It is necessary for us, as administrators, to recognize the characteristics of effective organizations. We must realize that schools are social units, in which we should strive for an environment that possesses the 21 characteristics listed in Figure 8-2, page 153.

Open up staff meetings where points of view are aired and discussed by everyone who is involved—support as well as professional staff. Good human relations skills practiced by everyone in the school are among the best time savers available.

Of course, the time-management techniques discussed in this book do not have to be used only by school administrators. Many of these techniques could be applied universally. After you become thoroughly familiar with them, we suggest you design a thorough in-service program for your staff to train them in appropriate time-management skills. The administration and the school staff, using similar time-management styles, will attain high efficiency.

Once long-range goals are established, keep them in mind. Try to use these to make daily decisions about how to use time with teachers and support staff. Recognize when you are spending too much time on something that is not helping move your staff toward the school's primary goals. This requires a conscious effort to monitor personal actions and time use as well as those of the staff. Develop a habit of thinking of the "big picture." This means you will have to consider broader conceptual implications of what you and your staff are doing. Do not waste time over mountains of trivia.

Be consistent and flexible. Talk with people about your style. Give examples to teachers that illustrate the way you tend to respond to problems or conflicts. Establish and discuss your

Figure 8-2

CHARACTERISTICS OF A HEALTHY ORGANIZATION

1. Objectives are widely shared and there is a strong and consistent flow of energy and time spent working toward these objectives.
2. People feel free to signal their awareness of difficulties because they expect the problems to be dealt with and they are optimistic that they can be solved.
3. Problem solving is highly pragmatic.
4. Organizational level as such is not considered a factor in determining the points of decision making.
5. There is a noticeable sense of team play in performance, planning, and discipline (shared responsibility).
6. The judgment of people lower down in the organization is respected.
7. The range of problems tackled includes personal needs and human relations.
8. Collaboration is freely entered into.
9. Conflicts are considered important to decision making and personal growth. They are dealt with in the open.
10. When there is a crisis, the people quickly band together to work until the crisis departs.
11. Joint critique of progress is routine.
12. Relationships are honest.
13. Leadership is flexible, shifting in style and purpose to suit the situation.
14. There is a high degree of trust among people and a sense of freedom and mutual responsibility.
15. Risk is accepted as a condition of growth and change.
16. Poor performance is confronted and a joint resolution sought.
17. Organizational structure, procedures, and policies are fashioned to help people get the job done and to protect the long-term health of the organization, not to give each bureaucrat his or her due.
18. There is a sense of order, and yet a high rate of innovation. Old methods are questioned and often give way to newer ones.
19. The organization itself adapts swiftly to opportunities or other changes because every pair of eyes is watching and every head is anticipating the future.
20. Frustrations are the call to action. "It's my/our responsibility to save the ship."
21. There is consistency between what is said and what is done.

expectations—and behave consistently with respect to them. One of the characteristics of a healthy organization is consistency between "what you say" and "what you do." Of course, you should be taking ethical and logical actions, but the *certainty* of your behavior as a leader in particular circumstances will prevent hesitancy of implementation by staff members.

HOW TO SAVE TIME WHEN WORKING WITH PEERS AND OTHER SYSTEM STAFF

Principals often find themselves placed on system-wide committees, study groups, or task forces. We feel being selected for such groups is an honor—a way of recognizing our skills. Too frequently, though, such assignments are given to a selected few. For those persons, these assignments become very time consuming and take away from their main responsibilities. Try to keep a balance between these outside activities and your role as a local school administrator. We recommended earlier that we all learn to say no to some requests. Estimate the amount of time that will be required for your involvement. Suggest other principals for such assignments—those who are quite capable·of accomplishing the tasks but, for a variety of reasons, are not asked.

If you are placed on a task force or committee, do not assume that other members of the group have the skills to organize and run meetings and other related tasks without direction. A great deal of time can be wasted in carrying out such projects by:

- waiting for someone to take the leadership role,
- waiting for someone to volunteer to do certain tasks, or
- waiting for someone to agree to have the next meeting, or to take notes, or to take care of the typing.

To save time (and you will not hurt feelings!), take the leadership role to organize and run the meetings or, at least, to help others do so. If you are assigned leader, list the goals of the project, develop a list of necessary subcommittees, identify the tasks to be performed, and prepare a tentative list of meeting dates, places, and times. Above all, plan the project so there is an ENDing time. All of us know of study groups, task forces, and the like that go on and on. We must all learn to recognize when the work is done or at the least, when our own contributions are no longer productive or needed. Do not kick a dead horse. When the work is finished, terminate the committee.

Have you ever closed the door to your office so you could do some planning? You sat and sat and thought and thought and no good ideas would come. You seem to have used all of your ideas and decide there is no solution to the problem or no new way of approaching it. This is an opportune time to seek help from a respected colleague.

Frequently some of our best ideas come to us after a discussion with peers. The most value we get from principal meetings is the breaks when we get together in small groups of our peers and talk about our jobs. To us, that is quality use of time.

Another valuable activity is peer observation. Take a day and shadow a fellow principal, taking as many notes as you are able. At the end of the day take time to discuss what occurred during the observation. Perhaps you will want to focus on particular aspects of time management or another singular activity or the day in general. A few days later, change roles and let your fellow principal shadow you.

Use your peers. Pick their brains and piggyback on their ideas. Establish friendships and a support system with them. The importance in developing and using such a support system can be seen in its helping to diffuse stress, in its giving you someone with whom to share problems or ideas, and in its giving you a setting for exploring further career or personal growth opportunities. The chart in Figure 8-3 will help you decide how to use a support system.

Figure 8-3

USING SUPPORT GROUPS

If you feel this:	Try this:
1. Social isolation	1. Share your joys and concerns with a peer.
2. Unacknowledged and not appreciated	2. List your strengths and accomplishments. Have a peer do the same thing for you. Compare them.
3. Emotional isolation	3. Work on developing a close friendship with a colleague.
4. Stimulus isolation	4. Get a peer to challenge your thinking and give you new ideas.
5. Powerlessness	5. Identify the formal and informal power and influence you actually have.
6. Job loneliness	6. Have a staff person as a confidant. Discuss in-school problems after setting limits.

Of course, support groups are not a cure-all, and unless carefully considered, can end up as time wasters rather than time savers. Some inherent problems of a support system could be:

- Size—the group from which we must select could either be too small or too large to fulfill the criteria in Figure 8-4, p. 156.

- Mix—we tend to seek people who are very much like ourselves while, in reality, it is better to have some diversity in the group.

- Advice—with a diverse group, we get different and often conflicting advice.

- Ideas—sometimes group members reinforce others' bad habits.

- Dependence—we may become so dependent on the group that we stop making any of our own decisions, or we may depend on one or two individuals too much for advice.

- Time—everyone is busy, so the support group may not be able to meet when help is needed.

Figure 8-4

CRITERIA FOR FORMING SUPPORT GROUPS

I. Interpersonal Relationships

    A. Willingness and ability to listen to each other
    B. Willingness and ability to ask each other for help
    C. Willingness and ability to give each other help
    D. Willingness to admit mistakes
    E. Desire to develop a trusting relationship

II. School District Criteria

    A. People from other schools or departments who can provide perspective
    B. People from other schools or departments who are most interdependent with your school
    C. People from other schools or departments who have goals similar to yours

---

WORKING WITH PARENTS AND OTHER COMMUNITY GROUPS— TIME WASTERS OR TIME SAVERS?

One time that is definitely not a time waster is when you are working with parents or other community groups. A major part of any job is working with the client group. If you become too aware of saving time when working with parents, you are liable to "ruffle feathers," missing opportunities for good public relations and probably spending a great deal of time undoing the damage.

Check back on your time log. In any given week, how many appointments did you have with parents or community groups such as the PTA? Were these appointments positive and constructive or were they negative? Were you forced into a defensive position? Were the parents dissatisfied? Do you see the need for the time-saving device commonly referred to as "public relations"? Time spent with parents and community members talking about the positive aspects of the school program, problem areas, and what is being done to resolve them, and plans for the future will result in minimizing time spent in negative conferences. Good public relations will not only save you time, but will also save time for the teachers.

How do we do this? Spend time finding out who the community leaders are and then work with the significant individuals and groups in the community. Who are the *few* who most heavily influence opinions about your school? Research in social community interaction calls such individuals "power actors," "knowledgeables," or "opinion leaders." According to Powers, these community leaders have tended to have the following characteristics: they are over 50 years old; they have higher than average income; they have power over credit, money, or jobs; they are better educated than others in the same age range; they are long-term community residents; they are self-employed, own their own business, or are executives; and they have access to needed resources.[1]

Find out what the parents want—their concerns, ideas, and suggestions. It is important to develop a close working relationship with parents and community. Community support for your school program is achieved only through hard work and spending time fostering a productive interchange between school and parent.

It is not our purpose here to write a book about school-community relations. However, it is our purpose to help you manage your time effectively. Time used for public relations is like making money—you have to spend some to save some.

We feel strongly that time spent establishing and maintaining positive feelings about schools will save time defending, justifying, and clarifying to individual community members. As administrators, we have used the following ideas at one time or another in our careers and found them to be quite workable.

Somewhere near your telephone, keep a 3″ × 5″ file box. Whenever you are on the telephone with a parent, or in conference, listen for the names of other community members. Each time you hear one, start a file card for that person. If the name is heard more than once, put a tally mark on the card. A pattern will begin to emerge of community members who may indeed be opinion leaders, and who now can be cultivated by you in your public relations efforts. Such a card file will take a minimum of time since it can be completed during your phone conversations.

Use parents to survey opinions and attitudes of other community members. Select a specific number of parents who would be willing to interview other community members—both parents and nonparents. This group of volunteers can also help you and your staff design the survey form. Assign a certain number of homes to each volunteer. The results will not be scientific in nature, but they will be very enlightening about community attitudes. By having parents do this, you will save immeasurable amounts of time.

You will need to be out of the building meeting with parents in their homes, at their churches or synagogues or in their clubs, attending "kaffeeklatches" or bridge groups. This role

---

[1]R. C. Powers. *Identifying the Community Power Structure.* (North Central Regional Extension Publication No. 19, NCRS-5 Leadership Series No. 2.) Ames, Iowa: Iowa State University of Science and Technology, 1965.

may be resisted by many principals because it "takes so much time." However, it really does not have to take more than one or two hours a month. Simply decide how often you should meet with small community groups for open discussions—every other week, every third week, once a month. Then, in PTA meetings, through newsletters, or through local newspapers, let it be known that you are interested in participating periodically in small groups to talk about schools and request hosts and hostesses. Once you have these names, have your secretary contact them for dates and let the hosts set up the meetings and invite the other participants. This way they feel involved and, best of all, they are using their time instead of yours to organize the sessions. The only time you need expend is the hour or two at the actual meeting. This has been by far the most successful public relations tool used by one of the authors, who is convinced it is a great timesaver by heading off problems before they actually arise.

Send a flyer home each week. This takes only a few minutes but is a regular opportunity to maintain contact with parents. The school menu, a list of significant events for the coming week, a comment about a school incident—these brief comments from you in a one-page, weekly newsletter can help foster understanding and community awareness. Figure 8-5, p. 159, is an example of such a letter.

Finally, follow four rules for good school public relations as given in a speech by John Wherry, Executive Director of the National School Public Relations Association.[2]

- Do a good job.
- Do a good job.
- Do a good job.
- Make sure people know you are doing a good job.

Developing and maintaining a good school-community relations program requires hard work. It also requires us to learn new skills and to be willing to get out of the building to meet parents on their own turf.

COMPLYING WITH FEDERAL, STATE, AND LOCAL LAWS
AND REGULATIONS WITHOUT UNDULY WASTING TIME

Death and taxes used to be the only two items we were sure would take some of our time. Now can be added, federal, state, and local regulations—and these *do* take time.

Our first suggestion about this is to do what the law says and you will not have to waste time:

- undoing it,
- standing trial, or
- going to jail.

Seriously, though, judgment, judgment, judgment must be used in determining the amount of time to be spent in complying with federal, state, and local regulations. By delaying

---

[2]J. Wherry. Speech given to the Montgomery County Public Schools, Maryland, Administrative and Supervisory Staff. January 14, 1981.

Figure 8-5

Weekly Letter to Parents

BES ELEMENTARY SCHOOL

February 27, 1982

Dear Parents:

Just a few items of interest this week. First, our enrollment appears to be gradually creeping upwards. We have picked up about 15 to 20 students in the past couple of weeks. From the information I can gather, I suspect we will have slow but steady growth the rest of this year and the next and then begin to grow rather rapidly. At this time there are approximately 300 living units under construction in the school community. It is difficult to say when these will be completed or exactly how many youngsters we will get from them.

On Tuesday evening at 7:30 the Parent Advisory Committee for Title I is sponsoring a reading workshop for parents. This workshop will be led by Miss Martin, one of our two very able reading teachers. We will meet in the library. Any interested parent is invited to attend. Please notify the office so we will know you are coming.

We have a very exciting cultural arts program coming up Wednesday morning of next week. Craig McKay, a mime, will present a show at 9:30 for the kindergarten through third grades and at approximately 10:10 for the upper grades. Mr. McKay will also be doing a program on March 24 for our next PTA meeting.

I have one concern with which I would like you to help us. Each morning it seems to me as if more children are being left off at school very early. School really does not begin until 9:00, and except for very bad weather conditions, the youngsters are not allowed in the building until 8:45. The early morning time from 8:30 to 9:00 is planning time for the teachers and as a consequence children who are here very early may not be supervised. We are not even expected to report to work officially until 8:30; however, those of us who come in early notice that there are many children already here—a few even as early as 7:30. I would ask your cooperation in not dropping your children off at school before 8:45 unless they are here for a very specific educational reason such as the FLES program or tutoring with a teacher.

Have a nice weekend.

Sincerely yours,

Sam Smith
Principal

complying immediately with some regulations, you may really end up wasting a large amount of time justifying your actions. On the other hand, using good judgment, you may make a low priority of some federal, state, or local regulation, knowing that you can fulfill that obligation at a different time.

Do not intentionally violate laws. All administrators should be aware of court actions regarding education. In the time you set aside for professional growth, read periodicals designed to keep you up-to-date on legislation and judicial actions so that you understand the consequences of noncompliance. Many educational associations provide legal information. So, too, might your own school system. Remember that we, as administrators, are responsible. Do not assume that the school district or your colleagues will protect you if what is being done is illegal. It is incumbent upon you to know where you stand—what are your rights and your liabilities.

Find out what is expected. Sometimes this is difficult because regulations and guidelines can be confusing and appear to be difficult to implement. Try to gain a perspective of the guidelines or regulations through the professional reading time we recommended earlier that you work into your daily schedule. Your own district may also have a particular point of view regarding legislative requirements. You should read and discuss these local interpretations thoroughly so you know what system expectations are.

Develop and use the time-management techniques to complete paperwork and reporting procedures for federal, state, and local laws and regulations. As always, remember to strive for *maximum* results from *minimum* use of time.

Keeping good records is especially important. Develop with your secretary an efficient filing system to keep track of all actions taken that relate to federal, state, or local regulations. Times change, different interpretations are made for legislative matters, so you should be sure to have complete records supporting all actions taken. Keep copies of requests made of you in this area and of all your responses. These simple steps will save much time if you are ever asked to document any of your actions.

CONCLUSION

Want to skip Chapter Eight's concepts? Oh, no! Reality says the people talked about in this chapter do in fact consume a great deal of our time—probably more than is justifiable. Generally, ignoring this results in time wasted "undoing." Remember, the goal of effective time managers is to use our time on high-priority items. Add the time saved using concepts in this chapter to time saved using concepts from the preceding seven chapters and you should be able to walk on down the road to the "Land of High Priorities"!

Chapter 9

Now You Can Design Your Own Time-Management System

*There's a proverb which says, "whatever you have, spend less";
this includes time, which should be used, not spent.—Anonymous*

INTRODUCTION

You have now completed the first eight chapters, and we hope you have enjoyed the book and received many meaningful time-management tips. Just how do you form your own time-management plan and make worthwhile use of all these concepts? In this final chapter we will review major concepts from the other eight chapters and remind you of timesavers—some of which you may already be implementing.

STEP A: BRILLIANT IDEAS FROM IMMEDIATE RECALL

As soon as you finish this book, turn back to the Contents and, using this to prod your memory, make a chart of the ideas that immediately come to mind as good ones for you. Figure 9-1, p. 162, is an example of a completed chart. If the Contents does not help in the recall, skim the book or use the notebook you have been keeping. When you have completed your chart, let it sit on your desk for at least two days but not more than three days. Then, reread it.

Now, try to decide whether you have too many items to start implementing or whether you do not have enough to make any difference. Attempting implementation of too many new ideas at one time may result in doing each of them poorly. Selecting too few new ideas may result in not enough positive change to result in a noticeable saving of time. A balance must be reached between the two. A magic "correct" number cannot be given. Only you can decide what is right for your own style and needs. Either way, go on now to the more formal procedure suggested in Steps B through E.

Figure 9-1

TIME-MANAGEMENT TECHNIQUES I LIKED

TECHNIQUE	WHO'S INVOLVED	WHEN TO DO IT	WHO'S MAINLY RESPONSIBLE—WHAT RESOURCES ARE NEEDED
Short-Term Planning	Self, Office Staff, Teachers	Every Monday at Staff Meeting	Self
Setting Goals	Self, Office Staff, Teachers	End of Year	Entire Staff
Establishing Deadlines	Self, Secretary, Others	Monday Mornings	Self, Secretary, Calendar
Daily "To Do" List	Self	Daily	Self—Yellow Pad
Drop-In Visitors	Secretary	Daily	Secretary, with My Support
In-Basket, Out-Basket	Self, Secretary	Daily	Secretary, Bins or Baskets
Paperwork	Self, Secretary	End of Day	Self, Secretary Folders (signature, action, to do, etc.)
SAME CHART 2 DAYS LATER			
Short-Term Planning	Self, Teachers	Every Monday— Staff Meeting	Teachers and Self
Daily "To Do" List	Self, Others	Daily End of Day for Next Day	Self, Secretary, Calendar and Yellow Pad

STEP B: LOOKING AT YOUR JOB AND HOW YOU DO IT

From the content of the first eight chapters we have selected several major concepts for your review as you proceed.

First, what *is* your job? Make a list of categories that represent its major dimensions. This should not be a detailed job description, just broad areas.

Using time logs, as illustrated in Chapters 1 and 3 and from your own notebook, look at how you spend your own time. How much is spent on the major dimensions you have listed? Review your major time wasters as identified in Chapter 1. Estimate the time lost, try to decide the cause, and think what can be done about it. Inclusion in your time-management notebook of a chart like that shown in Figure 9-2 will help structure this activity.

Look at the physical arrangement of your office, the filing system you use, the tasks done by your secretary and other office staff (as discussed in Chapter 2), and the responsibilities of other school personnel. Are all of these factors, human as well as material, organized to promote *EFFICIENCY*? Identify those that are not and make a list of them.

Examine the way you handle paperwork. Do you use an in-basket/out-basket? How often do you handle each piece of mail? Look at representative samples of your memos, letters, and reports. Is all this paperwork done *EFFICIENTLY*?

Review the way you handle your telephone communications. Is your life controlled by the telephone?

Figure 9-2

ELIMINATING MY TIME WASTERS

MY TIME WASTERS	ESTIMATE OF TIME LOST	WHY?	WHAT CAN I DO?
Drop-in Visitors	1 hour a day	Make myself too available	Improve scheduling; close door—all the way/part way
Telephone	25 minutes daily	Socializing	Stay on task; have calls better screened

Make a list of the number and kinds of meetings that you hold or in which you participate. List the purposes of these meetings and the number and types of people involved. Are these activities eating away at your time (as well as others')?

Finally, list the committees on which you serve, associations, school-community related groups, and task forces. How do these affiliations affect your time?

STEP C: LOOKING IN THE TIME MIRROR AT YOUR OWN TIME STYLE

Are you:

- The "be perfect" person who has to have everything done to perfection and cannot tolerate errors???

- The "work harder" type who comes in early and stays late, taking home a briefcase filled to the brim with materials to do at home at nights and on weekends???

- The "please others" person who never says no to any request and is *always* available to *everyone*???

- The "hurry up" person who arrives late for meetings only to leave early to get to another meeting that was scheduled back-to-back???

- The "be strong" type who is always "hanging tough" to get through the last and next crisis???

Think about the styles of others with whom you work. You need to be familiar with their styles to help you avoid conflict with them—a major time waster. Refer back to Chapter 1 for more details.

STEP D: AFTER DIAGNOSIS, JUST WHAT IS THE CURE?

Review your diagnosis from Steps A through C. Decide on those items that you can influence and control. Decide:

what you want to *start*,

what you want to *stop*, and

what you want to *continue*.

Now, get someone from your support system (as discussed in Chapter 8) to help. Ask this person to respond to your diagnosis and to help you make it more complete. Ask the person to give you new ideas and to react to your tentative choices of what to start, what to stop, and what to continue. Finally, ask the person to monitor your progress by meeting with you periodically as you implement your techniques.

STEP E: WHEN DO YOU DO IT?

Timing is of utmost importance. When do you start to implement major new ideas and techniques? It really is not important what time of year you attempt to do this as long as you lay the groundwork and do not suddenly develop drastic new modes of operation. For example, do not go one day from a complete "open-door" policy to a "closed-door—nobody-bother-me" policy the next day without explanation to your staff.

CONCLUSION

Each of us is different and in different surroundings. Only you can decide which time-management technique will work for you, and only you can adjust, rearrange, toss out, and rework these techniques to meet your situation. Whatever you decide, plan it carefully; keep it flexible; and be prepared to implement changes.

HAVE A GOOD TIME!

BIBLIOGRAPHY

Adams, J. D., et. al., *Transition: Understanding and Managing Personal Change*. London: Martin Robertson, 1976.

Benson, H., *The Relaxation Response*. New York: Morrow, 1975.

Bradford, L. P., Stock, D., and Horwitz, M., "How to Diagnose Group Problems." *Adult Leadership*, December 1953, 2(7).

Bradley, J. P., et. al, *The International Dictionary of Thoughts*. Chicago: J. G. Ferguson Publishing Co., 1969.

Cannon, W. B., *The Wisdom of The Body*. New York: W. W. Norton, 1932.

Educational Sales Representatives Association of Maryland, District of Columbia, and Delaware, Inc., *Directory Educational Sales Representatives* (1979–1980).

Hampton, R., *Behavioral Concepts in Management*. Belmont, California: Dickinson Publishing Co., Inc., 1968.

Hersey, P. and Blanchard, K. H., *Management of Organizational Behavior: Utilizing Human Resources* (3rd ed.). Englewood Cliffs, N.J.: Prentice-Hall, Inc., 1977.

Howard, D., "Executive Workload—The Triumph of Trivia." *The Wall Street Journal*, August 13, 1968.

Isgar, T., "Conflict Resolution: A Ten-Step Process." *OD Practitioner*, 1977, 9, 1–3; 14–15.

Kahler, T. and Capers, H., "The Miniscript." *Transactional Analysis Journal*, 1974, 4(1), 26–42.

Lakein, A., *How To Get Control Of Your Time and Your Life*. New York: The New American Library, Inc., 1974.

Lewin, K., "Frontiers in Group Dynamics: Concept, Method, and Reality in Social Science; Social Equilibria and Social Change." *Human Relations*, 1947, 1, 5–41.

Mackenzie, R. Alec, *The Time Trap*. New York: American Management Assn., Inc., 1972.

Powers, R. C., *Identifying the Community Power Structure* (North Central Regional Extension Publication No. 19, NCRS-5 Leadership Series No. 2). Ames, Iowa: Iowa State University of Science and Technology, 1965.

Rowan, R., "Keeping the Clock From Running Out." *Fortune*, 1978, 98, 76–78.

Selye, H., *Stress Without Distress*. New York: J. B. Lippincott, 1974.

Selye, H., *The Stress of Life*. New York: McGraw-Hill, 1956.

Steinmetz, L., *The Art and Skill of Delegation*. Reading, Massachusetts: Addison-Wesley, 1976.

"Ways to Stop Wasting Time on the Job." *U.S. News and World Report*, March 5, 1979, pp. 60, 63.

Wedgewood, H. C., "Fewer Camels, More Horses." *Personnel*, July–August, 1967.

Wherry, J., Speech given to the Montgomery County Public Schools, Maryland, Administrative and Supervisory Staff. January 14, 1981.

INDEX